Banking Reform and the Federal Reserve 1863-1923

Banking Reform and the Federal Reserve

1863–1923

ROBERT CRAIG WEST

Cornell University Press

ITHACA AND LONDON

First published 1977 by Cornell University Press.
Published in the United Kingdom by Cornell University Press Ltd., 2–4 Brook Street, London W1Y 1AA.

International Standard Book Number 0–8014–1035–5
Library of Congress Catalog Card Number 76–28028
Printed in the United States of America by York Composition Co., Inc.
Librarians: Library of Congress cataloging information appears on the last page of the book.

Contents

6   Contents

Charts

Preface

Much effort has been expended exposing the deficiencies of Federal Reserve policy during the system's early years. Judged by the standards of modern central banking theory, early policy makers do not seem to have had a clear view either of their powers or of their responsibilities. Policies of the first ten years of the Federal Reserve often appear contradictory, and are difficult to explain.

In this book I attempt to shed some new light on the early years of the Federal Reserve System. Rather than working backward from what central bankers today know about the monetary sector and their ability to affect it, this study analyzes the system's first decade in the context of the thought of that period, and of what had preceded the Federal Reserve Act of 1913. The act was the result of a half century of reaction to a troubled banking sector, characterized often by panics and the general instability of banks, particularly of small country banks; the act was a response to particular American problems, some political, some economic. Neither the act itself nor the actions of the system created by it can be understood without knowledge of the reform movement that preceded it.

Two issues were paramount in the reform discussion and also in the early years of the system: determination of a basis for policy decisions and agreement on an acceptable structure for stabilizing the banking system. Debates on each matter became simplified as time passed. The debate over policy developed into the question of the legitimacy of the "real bills doctrine," and the debate about structure came down to a choice between centralization and decentralization.

A caveat should be inserted here. The term "real bills doctrine" can be used to describe a large and seemingly varied group of views. Almost all who were involved in the reform discussion accepted all or part of the credit theory implied by the real bills doctrine propounded by Adam Smith, Thomas Tooke, and other English writers. Though there were clearly different interpretations of the real bills doctrine, those who espoused it had one important view in common: they believed that bank credit should be based only on real production, which would generally be represented by short-term commercial bills. One of the great appeals of the real bills doctrine to some of its advocates was the notion that it yielded automatic regulation of credit and the money supply; theoretically, the role of bankers was passive. In a country like England, with a well-established credit system based on bills of exchange such as existed from 1800 to 1850, a real bills doctrine fitted in easily, but the financial system of the United States had not developed in a similar manner. As a result, there was much difference of opinion about the validity and the definition of a monetary policy based on the real bills doctrine. In practice, the difficulty with the real bills doctrine was that it was a very specific, narrow theory of banking, rather than a general one.

The first six chapters of my book discuss American financial and monetary history and the reform attempts which culminated in the passage of the Federal Reserve Act. The reform movement is pictured as a response to conditions in the American economy.

Chapters 7 through 10 deal with the reform theory behind the act, and discuss the first decade of the system's operation, including the effects of the international financial upheaval caused by World War I. Chapter 9 analyzes the operations of the Federal Reserve System on the basis of information about the reform movement developed in earlier chapters, and the commonly held idea that Federal Reserve policy relied on the real bills doctrine is shown to be spurious. Chapter 10 discusses the structural features of the system and the stresses which developed as different groups competed for power.

In completing this work I have acquired many debts. Part of the research was supported by a grant from the Graduate School of Northwestern University. Several libraries were immensely helpful during my research. This work began in the Documents Room of the Northwestern University Library, where the staff was unfailingly courteous, as was the staff of the Manuscript Collection of the Columbia University Libraries.

Information from the H. Parker Willis Collection is used by permission of Parker B. Willis and the Columbia University Libraries. The Board of Governors of the Federal Reserve System has given permission to quote from papers and addresses of system officials contained in their research library. Special thanks are due Carl Backlund, Archivist of the Research Library of the Federal Reserve Bank of New York, for his invaluable assistance during my visit to the New York Bank. The Benjamin Strong Collection was consulted with the permission of the Federal Reserve Bank of New York. I also extend my thanks to the Library of Congress for allowing me to view the J. Laurence Laughlin Papers.

I would like to thank John Adams, who read Chapters 7 and 8, and Dudley Dillard, who read Chapter 7, for their helpful comments. Robert Masson, Eric Jones, and Jonathan Hughes read the whole work and each effected substantial improvement; I am deeply grateful to them. I owe a special debt to Professor Hughes, who helped me begin this work and through his suggestions improved it immensely. My thanks also go to Gail Weichert, who typed the manuscript.

My greatest debt is to my wife, Susan, who gave me encouragement and served as a willing typist of earlier drafts. Because of that and more, this work is dedicated to her.

ROBERT CRAIG WEST

College Park, Maryland

Banking Reform and
the Federal Reserve
1863-1923

CHAPTER 1

American Banking, 1836-1908

The process of banking reform with which this book is concerned was the product of a unique environment. Outside this environment the process is difficult, if not impossible, to understand. Many American reformers themselves did not recognize the uniqueness of the experience; as a result their attempts to capitalize on the successful aspects of European banking often were ill advised. This chapter will briefly survey American banking practice and structure from the expiration of the Second Bank of the United States in 1836 to the passage of the Aldrich-Vreeland Act in 1908.

Banking Practice, 1836–1863

The passage of the National Currency Act in 1863 and the National Banking Act in 1864 marked the federal government's return to banking legislation after twenty seven years of state autonomy in this area. The years from 1836, when the charter of the Second Bank of the United States expired, to 1863 were the heyday of state banking. Some states, Missouri and Indiana for example, controlled and operated their banks. Others chartered banks which for the most part operated independently of the state government, at least of direct control. The quality of banking varied considerably among the states. The state-run banks in Missouri and Indiana and the independent state banking system in Louisiana were outstanding examples of good state banking (the State Bank of Indiana should not be confused with the later institution with a similar name—the Bank of the State of Indiana). The State Bank of Illinois and Michigan's independent free banking system were examples of bad banking. In fact, experience in the latter two states caused some states, Iowa for instance, to ban banking entirely. The bankruptcy of the State Bank of Illinois apparently had more influence on Iowa politicians than the solidity of the State Bank of Missouri.[1]

By the time of the Civil War there were literally thousands of state banks, issuing notes in thousands of varieties. The notes varied in value from par to near zero, depending on the financial strength and trustworthiness of the issuing bank. Notes which were perfectly good in one area might pass at a discount in another. Catalogues called bank note detectors collected information about the value of notes and provided some means of setting up exchange rates between the notes of different banks.

The many varieties of notes often made interregional trade difficult. It was difficult and expensive to redeem the notes of distant banks. The Suffolk System, which developed in New England, was one attempt by a larger bank to force other banks to issue sound notes. The Suffolk Bank refused to accept or pay out the notes of any bank outside Boston which did not maintain a redemption deposit in the Suffolk Bank. The

1. For a more extensive view of banking during this period see Davis R. Dewey, *State Banking before the Civil War* (Washington: GPO, 1910); Bray Hammond, *Banks and Politics in America: From the Revolution to the Civil War* (Princeton: Princeton University Press, 1957); and William G. Sumner, *A History of Banking in the United States* (New York: Journal of Commerce and Commercial Bulletin, 1896).

system was enlarged in 1824, when other important Boston banks joined. Any bank outside Boston which refused to maintain redemption deposits with the system faced the prospect of having all of its notes which found their way into Boston collected and returned for redemption in specie. Under this system New England's note issue became sounder, and by 1830 the note issue of Massachusetts banks was circulating at par.[2]

The threat of a large amount of notes being returned for redemption was a powerful force in restricting unsound note issues. As the Second Bank of the United States learned, it was also unpopular. Southern and western branches of the Second Bank of the United States were encouraged to substitute their bank notes for local state bank notes. The branches did this by returning state bank notes to the issuing bank for redemption in specie instead of paying them out to their own customers during normal business. The Second Bank of the United States hoped that its notes would eventually become the major portion of the currency and that some regularity in the currency would be achieved. In many areas banks were not capable of redeeming their notes in specie and therefore objected to this practice. No doubt they were part of the opposition to a renewal of the bank's charter.[3]

Fear of forced note redemption caused the formation of "wildcat banks," or banks whose offices were so deep in the wilderness that "only the wildcats could find them." Transportation difficulties and lack of information afforded ample opportunity for unscrupulous operators to turn a quick profit by

2. Dewey, *State Banking before the Civil War*, pp. 82–86; Hammond, *Banks and Politics*, pp. 549–556; John Jay Knox, *A History of Banking in the United States* (New York: Kelly, 1969; originally published 1903), pp. 365–368.

3. Hammond, *Banks and Politics*, chap. 14; Peter Temin, *The Jacksonian Economy* (New York: Norton, 1969), chap. 2.

circulating unbacked currency. This could be done by issuing notes and spending or loaning them some distance away (even in another state), causing a substantial delay before they were redeemed. Some might never be returned, and the probability that a large number of notes would be returned at any one time was small if they were spread over a wide enough area. Banking practice of this sort was a major reason for the ban on banking written into some state constitutions.[4]

The National Banking Act

The National Banking Act of 1864 (which superseded the National Currency Act) was viewed by some as an attempt to impose order on the chaotic state of American banking. Others saw the act as a means of creating a reliable market for government bonds. Whatever the reasons for the act's passage, it marked an important step forward in banking reform.[5]

The concept behind the establishment of the national banks was one commonly called commercial banking. In commercial banking, as distinguished from investment banking, a bank limits itself to short term commercial lending. In some cases longer-term investments are made, but these investments are made using only the bank's capital rather than money on current account. In the United States this type of banking is best exemplified by the Louisiana state banking system set up in 1842. The Louisiana Banking Act required all banks to separate long- and short-term loans. Restrictions were placed on the

4. Hammond, *Banks and Politics,* pp. 605–617. Also see references in note 2.

5. Andrew McFarland Davis in a report prepared for the National Monetary Commission, *The Origin of the National Banking System* (Washington: GPO, 1910), stresses the creation of a stable nationwide currency as the bill's primary purpose, although it was and is generally accepted that the main reason for the act's passage was to strengthen the credit of the United States.

increase of long-term debt. Short-term debt, generally ninety-day commercial paper, was not renewable. Sanctions were imposed against those who failed to pay their debts and even against those who asked to have credit renewed. The Louisiana Banking Act of 1842 is one of the few state or national banking acts before 1913 which has received widespread approval.[6]

While the restrictions on national banks were not as strict as those in the Louisiana law, the banks were prohibited from engaging in certain actions. They were allowed to invest in real estate to satisfy only their own needs for banking facilities. Other long-term, noncommercial operations were forbidden. This ban had a great deal to do with the later rise of state banks and trust companies. Even though the authors of the National Banking Act were not willing to go as far as the Louisiana act, it is obvious that their idea of a bank more nearly approximated a commercial bank than an investment bank.

There were some problems encountered in engaging in this type of banking in the postbellum United States. In many agricultural areas, especially around New Orleans, commercial finance was based on short-term paper. In the North, on the other hand, the Civil War had fostered the development of cash payments in commercial transactions. This grew from the practice of offering discounts to purchasers who payed for goods in cash. Businessmen took advantage of these offers by applying to their banks for short-term loans if the cash discount was greater than the interest charge.[7] Where single-name notes were used in this practice, they were the economic

6. See Sumner, A History of Banking, pp. 387–391; Hammond, Banks and Politics, pp. 680–685; and Fritz Redlich, The Molding of American Banking (New York: Hafner, 1947), II, 32–65.

7. See Margaret G. Myers, The New York Money Market (New York: Columbia University Press, 1931), chap. 15.

equivalent of the two-name commercial paper commonly used in European financial systems. Unfortunately, some banks made short-term loans to customers and then repeatedly renewed these loans at maturity. For this reason, it was often difficult for banks discounting such notes to distinguish between single-name commercial paper and single-name paper which was continually renewed to support long-term investment. A bank might actually be far less liquid than its portfolio would indicate. In many cases this practice allowed banks to circumvent the intent of the law. Part of the argument for reform during the early twentieth century was for standardized note discounting procedures in order to correct this problem.

Fritz Redlich argues that the National Banking Act of 1864 was influenced by the English Bank Act of 1844 and the thought of Lord Overstone, its principal proponent.[8] He traces the influence through Senator John Sherman, who was persuaded by bankers Jay and Henry Cooke to support Secretary of the Treasury Salmon P. Chase in his attempts to secure the passage of the National Banking Act. Redlich offers two pieces of evidence in the 1864 act: the limitation on the total amount of notes which could be issued by the banks as a whole, and the separation of issuing and redemption functions. Both are features of the English Bank Act of 1844. Although Sherman demonstrated a general knowledge of foreign banking systems, especially the French and English, he made no direct reference at the time to any relationship between the English Bank Act of 1844 and the National Banking Act of 1864. The fact that all references given by Redlich comparing the two acts date from the middle 1870's might indicate that any similarity between the two bills was seen only after the fact. The limitation on note issues probably should be attributed to the fear of overissue, a major problem over the thirty years prior to the passage

8. Redlich, *Molding of American Banking*, II, 105.

of the National Banking Act.[9] The second piece of evidence is
hardly evidence at all. Even though it is true that a separate
redemption agency was set up, the notes were issued through
those banks which also were required to redeem them. The
functions of the Issue Department of the Bank of England and
the Treasury's redemption fund bore little resemblance to one
another.

The philosophy of bank regulation found in the National
Banking Act is basically the same as that behind the New
York State banking act of 1838. New York State had suffered
for years under a particular evil: the requirement of a special
state charter for bank organization. In 1838 the state legisla-
ture passed a banking law embodying the principle which became known as free banking. Monopoly practice and special
favoritism had been rampant under the old law, and it was felt
that competition would relieve these problems. The National
Banking Act extended free banking under federal charter to
the entire nation. Charters were granted to any group of five or
more people who could meet the minimum capital requirements contained in the law. In fact, the comptroller of the
currency, a new official created by the act to oversee the
system, was allowed some discretionary power concerning
charters. In general, applicants were required to demonstrate
some need for the bank and to possess the proper character and
intentions, rather subjectively evaluated criteria. Insufficient
bank capital had been an important problem in many states
and because of this, minimum capital requirements were set
out in the act. The minimum capital requirements were intended to ensure that banks possessed a capital commensurate
with the amount of business they were expected to acquire. At

9. See John Sherman, *Selected Speeches and Reports on Finance
and Taxation* (New York: Appleton, 1879), pp. 60–61.

least half of a national bank's capital was to be paid in before the bank was allowed to open for business.

The National Banking Act authorized national banks to issue a new type of bank note backed by certain United States government bonds. National banks could not issue notes until they had deposited with the comptroller of the currency a specified amount of bonds bearing a circulation privilege. Bond-secured note issues were not new, but earlier issues had not usually been backed by United States government bonds and were therefore less secure if the note issuer went bankrupt.

To ensure that noteholders would be adequately protected, the National Banking Act restricted the note issue of the national banks to 90 percent of the bonds' market value, not to exceed 90 percent of par value. This restriction was later raised to 100 percent of par value when United States government bonds were selling consistently above par in the market. The act also included a provision aimed at distributing the notes evenly across the country. However, fewer national bank notes were issued in the West than in the East, and after the end of the Civil War few national bank notes were issued in the South. This was a problem since banking institutions were less developed in the West and South. Payments depended on bank notes rather than checking deposits to a far greater extent than in the East.

The note issue of any national bank was limited to the amount of its paid-in capital. This limitation was intended to correct a particular abuse under many state banking laws. Some banks used specie to buy the bonds of a state government, but the actual specie payment might be only a certain percentage of the bonds' market value (such bonds were often sold at a discount anyway). The bonds would be deposited with the state government, and the bank would receive notes equal to the par value of the bonds which it would then use to complete the payment. The surplus of note issue equal to the original specie capital (or even more if the bonds were at a discount in the market) could be used to repeat the process. In this manner, some banks were able to maintain a circulation equal to twenty or thirty times their paid-in specie capital. Often the interest received on the bonds deposited with the state government exceeded the bank's actual capital by a substantial amount.[10]

The idea of bond-secured currency, as is obvious from the description of state banking practice, was not innovated by the authors of the National Banking Act. Part of the Bank of England's issue was "backed" by government debt, the so-called fiduciary issue. On the whole, however, the tendency was for bank notes to be backed either by specie (as were Bank of England note issues above the fiduciary limit), by commercial bills (as in the case of the notes of English country banks),[11] or a combination of the two (such as the case of German commercial banks). The only specie backing for national bank notes was the Treasury's 5 percent redemption fund.

The National Banking Act also standardized the reserves held against bank deposits by making them uniform with respect to the size and location of the national banks. Under most state banking laws, reserves were either unregulated or low percentages were required. In some cases state bank reserves amounted only to till money, and therefore the banks

10. See Hammond, *Banks and Politics*, chap. 19, for a more complete description of banking practices in the United States during the period 1830–1865.

11. After the Bank Act of 1844, the tendency in England was toward specie backing, as the Bank of England absorbed the note issue of country banks which were encouraged to give up their note issue power. This was possible because of the rapid rise in the use of checking deposits as a means of payment. The deposits granted by the country banks were still backed by commercial paper.

were incapable of meeting even the slightest increase in demand for hand-to-hand currency. Under the new act, reserve requirements were based on the location of the bank: highest for banks in New York City and lowest for country banks. Banks outside New York City were allowed to count deposits in certain other banks as part of their reserves.

The word "reserve" as used in the National Banking Act is really a misnomer. Since banks tended to be "loaned up" and thus always near their minimum reserve ratio, the amounts held in bank vaults or on deposit with other banks were not available to meet sudden demands without violating the law. Banks were induced by the profit motive to approach their minimum reserves but were forbidden by law to go below them. In stringent situations, banks were forced to contract credit to gain liquidity, since the punishment for violating their reserve requirements might be closure by the comptroller of the currency.

In practice, reserve levels were computed as averages over a certain period, generally weekly or biweekly, depending on the location of the bank. Therefore, reserves could be drawn down over short periods if the bank expected excess reserves from net deposits in the near future. Receivership was a threat only after a thirty-day period of deficient reserves. Up to that time the bank was merely prohibited from making new loans or paying dividends. In such cases the pressure on the banks to contract loans was all the more powerful.

This description is by no means a complete one, but the important points have been covered. One final note: the "system" described above was not really a system at all. There was no mechanism for interbank cooperation. The only existing cooperative mechanism was the requirement that every bank outside New York City name a redemption agent for its notes. This reflected New York's emergence as the primary financial center in the United States. A country bank could name a bank in New York City or in one of the listed cities. A bank in a listed city was required to name a New York City bank as redemption agent. Banks in New York City were to act as their own redemption agents. This requirement lowered the costs of redemption to noteholders but was of little use in times of crisis.

The National Banking Act did not even cover all the banks. In fact, by 1913, there were twice as many state banks as national banks, although the total deposits of the two groups were roughly equal. The government made an attempt to eliminate state banks in 1865 when Congress passed a bill placing a prohibitive tax on state bank note issues. This measure was not popular (it passed the House of Representatives by only one vote) and was also unsuccessful. After a few years of decline, state banks returned to occupy an important position in American banking. This was possible because state banks quickly learned that note issues were becoming less important relative to demand deposits as the financial system developed. As a result, their business could be continued without the power of note issue.

The National Banking Act was important because, more than anything else, it determined the nature of banking from 1863 to 1913. Three aspects of the act were of paramount importance: the philosophy of independent unit banks, the type of note issue, and the reserve structure. Debate over these three issues was to form the core of the banking reform discussion.

The Treasury and the Banks

During this period the United States Treasury exerted a great deal of power in the financial system. The Independent Treasury was set up in 1846 to separate government revenue collection and disbursements from the banking system. Before that time, certain "pet" banks had been the chief depositories of federal funds. One purpose behind the Independent Treasury was to remove this element of favoritism from the United States government's finances. The National Banking Act made national banks legal depositories for internal revenue funds but not for customs duties; these were to remain in the vaults of the Subtreasuries.

Before the 1860's the separation of government funds from the banking system had a negligible effect on the financial system because their size relative to the total volume of financial transactions was small. After the Civil War, government revenues and disbursements grew until they were no longer relatively minor sums. Problems often arose since the banks' liquidity needs did not always coincide with the government's disbursements—chiefly quarterly payments on the national debt.

The dual fact that customs duties were payable only in gold and were not eligible for deposit in the national banks was important to the New York money market. An increased demand for gold to pay customs duties would draw down the reserves of New York banks, and during times of stringency, this pressure had drastic effects. Often the Treasury came to the banks' aid. The Treasury sometimes prepaid or simply purchased bonds to free surplus funds. The Treasury also sold gold to stabilize its price and provide lawful money for reserves. Some evidence indicates that during later years the banks may have expected the Treasury to come to their aid. They were therefore willing to engage in less conservative practices than might have been indicated by the general business situation. While the Treasury could and sometimes did provide aid in times of panic during the period 1863–1907, the working of the Independent Treasury System was not keyed to the nation's financial needs. Often the banks and the

Treasury worked at cross-purposes and impeded smooth functioning of the financial sector.[12]

Crises in Banking

The financial structure which developed had a very difficult time reacting to shocks in the economy. The years from 1863 to 1913 were marked by periodic crises. Major crises occurred in 1873, 1884, 1893, and 1907. While the causes of each crisis were different, their effects on the financial structure tended to be very similar.[13]

In 1873, Jay Cooke and Company, an important private banking house, failed because of problems in railroad investments. At that time the company was probably the best-known banking firm in the United States because of the bond sale campaigns they had handled during the Civil War. The result of the failure was a run on all the banks and eventual suspension when the banks found themselves unable to meet their depositors' demands for cash. Loan certificates were issued by many clearinghouses to economize on cash in interbank payments, and to ease the pressure the government deposited funds in some of the banks. In New York, though not in other cities, banks pooled their reserves to meet demands for currency when and where they occurred. After the crisis was over, several reports suggested some changes in bank practices, but no legislative action was taken. Inaction was probably caused

12. For a more complete discussion of the Treasury's operations vis-à-vis the banks, see David Kinley, *The Independent Treasury of the United States and Its Relation to the Banks of the Country* (Washington, D.C.: GPO, 1910), and Ester Rogoff Taus, *Central Banking Functions of the United States Treasury, 1789–1941* (New York: Columbia University Press, 1943).

13. For a contemporary view of the crises discussed here, see O. M. W. Sprague, *History of Crises under the National Banking System* (New York: Kelly, 1965; originally published in 1910).

by a general agreement that the system would work if banks would pursue more conservative policies.

The panic of 1884 was primarily confined to New York City and was a reflection of some bad business practices. The banks of the city took action immediately, and the crisis was over within a week. However, the reserve pooling which occurred during the previous panic was not considered in 1884 because of the relative mildness and short duration of the crisis. Such a refusal indicated an attitude which was to cause problems in the future.

Although a stringency occurred in 1890, the next severe panic occurred in 1893. It was the result of many causes, and no single one can be considered crucial. Bank practice had not changed in any substantial way over the preceding two decades, and banks found themselves in a position similar to those of previous years. However, after 1884, banks under pressure seemed to resort more readily to suspension. The skill with which problems were handled seems to have declined rather than improved. The banks apparently failed to learn from past experience. O. M. W. Sprague, a contemporary economist, maintained that the situation in 1907 when the difficulty began was probably the least serious of the four major crisis periods, but was allowed to "drift into the most complete interruption of . . . banking facilities that the country has experienced since the Civil War."[14]

The situation was no doubt worsened by the crisis psychology imparted to the public. Bank customers believed that their demands for payment could not be met in emergencies and knew that with each crisis some banks failed, an attitude that made the situation worsen rapidly as depositors and other creditors attempted to make good their claims on the banks. While bankers as a whole may have realized that normal cash positions would not always be adequate, they seem to have

14. Ibid., p. 319.

been unwilling to practice conservative policies which would have given them a margin of safety.

A View of the Problems: Organization and Currency

Contemporaries were able to see many of the National Banking Act's shortcomings. From their point of view these problems fell into two categories: problems of organization (or lack of it), and problems with the "inelasticity" of note issues under the National Banking Act. The first problem took many forms, including scattered reserves, lack of clearing facilities, and the absence of a lender of last resort. The second problem dealt with the inability of the circulating currency to expand when needed, that is, before there was a run on the banks.

Some organizational features of the National Banking Act prevented smooth operation of the financial system. The National Banking System was not really a system at all but rather a loose body of independent banks responsible only to themselves and responsible only for themselves. This condition effectively proscribed any united action among the banks when abnormal conditions prevailed. The reserve system written into the National Banking Act has always been considered defective. A serious pyramiding of reserves was caused by allowing some banks to count deposits in other banks as part of their reserves. The actual level of available reserves was much lower than was nominally required. The system was always weaker than it appeared and less able to meet any increased demand for hand-to-hand currency relative to demand deposits.

Some New York banks, in order to increase their share of interbank deposits, paid interest on demand deposits. This practice was a source of trouble since reserve deposits became concentrated in a few banks.[15] The banks engaged in this practice were obliged to lend out the money to obtain a return with which to pay the interest. Or to look at it from the other

15. Ibid., pp. 20–24.

side, the banks saw profit opportunities which exceeded the interest charge they would be required to pay to attract deposits and therefore profited on the margin between the two rates. The money obtained in this manner was generally loaned on the stock exchange in the form of "call loans." These loans were presumed to be almost perfectly liquid since the funds were available on call. This was indeed true when only one bank was attempting to call its loans. In that case, the loan would most likely be shifted to another bank or banks. However, a certain level of call loans was normally outstanding, and any attempt by a number of banks to call loans at the same time would cause a sharp disturbance in the stock market because the loans could not be shifted. If severe enough, this disturbance might lead to the suspension of trading on the stock market, making all call loans uncollectable. For this reason call loans were the least liquid type of loan in times of stress.

Often, after a period of stability, banks approached their minimum reserve requirements as they attempted to maximize profits. Because of reserve pyramiding and individual bank isolation during a crisis, it became impossible for banks to redeem an abnormal amount of deposits without a credit contraction. Two separate factors enter here. First, a stringency placed on country banks affected all banks because of the reserve system. Second, stringencies tended to snowball since no effective means of interbank cooperation existed. The first problem is obvious, given the structure of the reserve system. When country banks called deposits from their correspondent banks in cities other than New York, those banks were often forced to call deposits from New York. Banks subjected to calls were forced to restrict credit if they lacked free reserves. Banks were reluctant to go below their minimum required reserves to meet a sudden demand because of the legal sanctions which might be imposed, for banks did not violate their reserve requirements except in the severest circumstances. The only recourse was a credit contraction. Second, there was no cooperative arrangement through which strong banks could come to the aid of weaker banks, stopping the clamor for cash at once. Reserves were too scattered to be of general use. Instead, the panic generally spread from weaker to stronger banks as all became suspect.

The proper reaction would have been for the banks on which the demands were first made to dip below their required reserves. They could do this because over the long run money would flow back and their reserves would be replenished. Stronger or less troubled banks should have come to the aid of others and loaned reserves to satisfy the demand. But reserves, just as is the case even today, under the National Banking Act were not reserves at all, and for this reason such action was difficult for a bank to undertake on its own.

The absence of a general cooperative organization made the situation even more difficult. A bank which came to the aid of others was likely to lose reserves to other banks. In a world of every bank for itself, actions which were proper for all the banks as a group became suicidal for any individual bank. Because of the development of clearinghouses, things were not quite as bad as they might have been. In both 1873 and 1907 it is probable that the crises would have been worse had not New York banks come to one another's aid. In other cities the situation was less admirable. Nevertheless, the clearinghouses allowed some cooperation during panics. They also convinced many people that more cooperation would improve the operation of the financial sector.

Although clearinghouses operated regularly, clearing checks and drafts and transacting other interbank business, during crises they took on added importance. During times of stringency, they issued clearinghouse loan certificates based on the assets of member institutions. These certificates were used in place of currency in interbank clearings. Therefore, bank reserves were increased by the amount of lawful money ordinarily tied up in clearing procedures. While the loan certificates could not be counted as reserves, they freed cash by serving as a substitute in interbank payments.[16]

In 1873 and 1907, New York banks pooled their reserves to meet the demand for currency. In 1873 they did so as a part of the agreement which set up clearinghouse loan certificates. In later years banks were reluctant to cooperate and in 1884 and 1893 they did not. Pooling was accomplished in 1907 because of the pressure exerted on New York bankers by J. P. Morgan. These cooperative actions during panics impressed many people and influenced later legislation. Also, the reluctance with which banks engaged in such operations demonstrated the need for outside regulation of bank activities.

Currency problems, the second category, were generally combined into one: the note issue's lack of responsiveness to the currency needs of the economy, generally called the inelasticity of the currency. At that time, hand-to-hand currency was composed of national bank notes, United States Treasury Notes, gold coin and certificates, silver coin and certificates, and other subsidiary currency. The amount of silver currency, both coin and certificates, was fixed, as were United States Treasury Notes. Gold coin and certificates were allowed to grow as the amount of monetary gold grew. Subsidiary coins and national bank notes were slightly flexible, since they were allowed to grow under the law (the maximum limit on national bank notes having been raised from the initial limit of $300,000,000). The elasticity problem, however, did not concern the long-run growth of the money supply but rather a short-term expansion and contraction.

16. For a more complete view of the operation of clearinghouses during this period, see James Graham Cannon, *Clearing Houses* (Washington, D.C.: GPO, 1919), and Sprague, *History of Crises*.

At each crisis, the demand for currency could not be met without drawing down reserves, since in the short run national banks were not able to expand the supply of national bank notes. This was particularly true during later periods when United States government bonds were selling at a premium of 40 percent or more. To expand their issue of national bank notes, banks would have had to give up 40 percent more in lawful money (gold, gold certificates, and so forth) than they would have received in national bank notes when the bonds they purchased were deposited with the Treasury, since note issues were limited to the par value of the bonds. In such a case, the money supply actually would have decreased by 40 percent.

There would have been a further decrease if the lawful money used to purchase government bonds had been held as reserves. If the reserve ratio of a bank was 25 percent, the use of a dollar of reserves to purchase a dollar of government bonds would decrease reserves by one dollar. Deposits would have to decrease by four dollars in order to increase national bank notes by one dollar. With a lower reserve ratio or a premium on government bonds, the decrease would be greater.

In addition to periodic stringencies during panics, there were also regular stringencies each year in the fall when farmers were harvesting and moving crops. The most common contemporary explanation was that the agricultural areas of the United States were in general the most backward in terms of their financial development. This does not mean that they lacked a financial structure but rather that extensive commercial relations, especially the wide use of checking deposits, had not developed to the same extent in these areas as they had in large cities. This characteristic, combined with the distinct seasonality of business in these regions, was most often given as the reason for the sharp seasonal increase in the demand for hand-to-hand currency.[17] For this reason, the problem with the inelasticity of the currency was frequently described as a problem with the varying acceptability of media of exchange.

Given the nature of the problems as they were seen during the National Banking era, their solution appeared obvious to contemporary writers on monetary matters. The problems fell into two classes, each of which anticipates one of our issues. The note issue problem provided fertile ground for the development of an acceptance of the real bills doctrine. There was little understanding of the true nature of the problem and the discussion concentrated on problems with the note issue rather than problems with credit. The lack of an effective reserve system or mechanism for cooperation began the trend toward the reinstitution of federal government control and a more structured form of organization. This latter trend was opposed by the belief in a free and independent banking system.

17. This is the contemporary view given by writers such as Sprague, *History of Crises*, and E. W. Kemmerer, *Seasonal Variations in the Relative Demand for Money and Capital in the United States* (Washington, D.C.: GPO, 1910). A more recent view and a revision of the older studies can be found in C. A. E. Goodhart, *The New York Money Market and the Finance of Trade, 1900–1913* (Cambridge: Harvard University Press, 1968). Goodhart traces the cause of the autumn money flow from the East to the West and South to the large trade surplus which these latter two regions built up as crops were moved to the urban areas. Likewise, the reverse flow in spring and summer is traced to a trade deficit on the part of the West and South. In other words, the flows observed by contemporaries in the fall were not caused by an increase in the transaction demand for money in the West and South, but by an increase in the demand for agricultural goods in the East. The movement of funds to the East in spring and summer occurred not because they could find no profitable occupation at home, but rather because a trade deficit developed in the rural areas. The excess demands for (supplies of) money reflected excess supplies of (demands for) goods. See Goodhart, *New York Money Market*, pp. 4–8.

CHAPTER 2

Reform Proposals, 1863-1908

This chapter is concerned primarily with proposals made during 1863–1908 which were intended to make the existing "system" work better. Proposals generally fell into one of two categories: those which dealt only with the medium of exchange problem, and those which made some attempt to deal with the question of organization as well. Proposals in the latter category represented a more mature view of monetary matters, since there was substantial interaction between the two problems. Early attempts to deal with organizational matters did not go very far. For the most part the existing banking structure was to be left unchanged, although some proposals suggested new appendages. Serious attempts at organizational change were not made until the twentieth century. The most important consequence of the early reform proposals was the beginning of wide acceptance of the real bills doctrine. In this period the concept was still in a very rudimentary stage; it was nothing more than the idea that notes should be based on the assets of the banks.

The First Wave, 1863–1893

Suggestions for banking reform appeared early in the National Banking era. Some of these plans proposed substantial change; others aimed only at small changes in banking practice, which nonetheless might have had a major impact on the stability of the financial system.

The periods of widest debate on banking reform are found immediately following the major financial upheavals of the National Banking era. The correlation between panics and reform attempts should not be particularly surprising, since underlying all banking discussion was the unspoken belief that the banking "system" (actually the lack of a system) of the United States was sound and proper. Therefore a climate conducive to discussion of reform did not exist unless the economy had recently been subjected to a crisis. Even when discussion occurred, it was not always aimed at the "system" itself but rather at individual bank practice, especially during the early years of the National Banking era. After 1863 and the fall of the Second Bank of the United States, support for competitive banking was widespread and important in banking development. Many state banking laws, but most particularly the National Banking Act, reflect this fact. During the five decades after 1863, the concept of competitive banking experienced no substantial challenge. None of the proposals discussed in this chapter offered any alternative to the atomistic banking style which typified American finance. Nevertheless, a distinct evolution in the nature of the proposals can be seen.

In the beginning, proposals were aimed primarily at bank practice rather than at basic theoretical or organizational issues. It was recognized that the National Banking Act's reserve provision was a cause of instability especially since some banks paid interest on demand deposits. The banks engaged in this practice were able to garner almost all the interbank deposits held as reserves.

Shortly after the 1873 crisis, Secretary of the Treasury William A. Richardson came out very strongly against interest payments on demand deposits.[1] He asked Congress to pass legislation prohibiting national banks to engage in such a "pernicious" practice. He noted that Congress was helpless to proscribe such interest payments by state banks, but he at least wished to save national banks from financial "embarrassment."

The New York Clearing House Committee also recommended that banks refrain from paying interest on demand deposits.[2] However, the banks could not reach unanimous agreement on this matter. Since it was felt that without such agreement a proscription could not be effectively adopted, action on this question was dropped; the banks had failed in an important attempt to police themselves. This topic returned each time the volatile nature of the National Banking Act's reserve structure showed itself.

Most discussion of the reserve problem centered on the practice of paying interest on deposits, although such payments were the natural outgrowth of competitive free banking. The real difficulty was not that banks paid interest on deposits, but that the law allowed interbank deposits to be counted as reserves. It was the special nature of these deposits which created instability in the banking system.

Under the National Banking Act, country banks, which experienced the greatest demand for currency in times of stress, were subject to a lower reserve requirement than banks in more highly developed areas where credit relations were largely substituted for currency. Under the National Banking Act, country banks were required to have on hand reserves equal to 9 percent of their deposits, obviously far too low a

1. William A. Richardson in *Annual Report on the State of the Finances* (Washington, D.C.: GPO, 1873), pp. iii–xxxix.
2. Sprague, *History of Crises*, pp. 91–104.

requirement given the nature of banking and finance. In 1863, when Secretary of the Treasury Chase asked George S. Coe, a prominent New York banker, to discuss the proposed National Currency Act with his fellow bankers in New York prior to its introduction into Congress, Coe was so opposed to the plan that he refused. He did suggest that the bill should require all banks to maintain a 20 to 25 percent reserve in coin.[3] This was a conservative New York banker speaking in favor of strong reserves held completely within the vaults of each bank. About ten years later, Coe, as chairman of the New York Clearing House Committee, recommended that interest payments on deposits be discontinued so that banks would have no incentive to hold reserves anywhere but their own vaults, therefore exerting less demand on other banks during times of stress.[4]

Many country banks kept deposits in city banks for clearing purposes and to redeem notes. City banks outside New York also kept deposits in New York banks for the same purposes. Some state bank laws allowed deposits held in certain specified banks to be counted as reserves by state banks. If the National Banking Act had not legitimized this common practice, deposits held for clearings or convenience would not have been legal reserves, and a bank's earning power would have been lowered by the amount of deposits it found necessary to hold in other banks. Profits were at issue and those who took the view that interest payments on demand deposits should be abolished represented the conservative side. Interbank deposits benefited country banks through conveniences such as clearing and city banks because of the increased lending power such deposits allowed. Since it benefited all banks to maintain interbank

3. Redlich, *Molding of American Banking*, p. 103.
4. Sprague, *History of Crises*, pp. 91–95.

deposits, the argument centered around the interest payments on demand deposits. Country banks wished to receive some return on deposits which they were in most cases obliged to keep. On the other hand, city banks wished to be relieved from a competitive situation through legislation which would prohibit interest payments on deposits. If interest payments were stopped, out-of-town deposits might tend to spread themselves more evenly among the banks and the funds would be available to city banks at zero or at least very low cost.

Although the abolition of interest payments on demand deposits held center stage in the early discussions, two other problems were also recognized. In the Finance Report of 1873, Secretary Richardson recommended changes in the National Banking Act's reserve provisions. Richardson felt that "to allow national banks to use part of their reserves at seasons of the greatest pressure, under proper restrictions and regulations, would afford some flexibility." He went on to say that banks in redemption cities "might do much to give steadiness and safety, if they were authorized . . . to exercise a large discretion in the use of their reserves, in the rate of interest to be charged at different seasons and under different circumstances, and in other matters, within limits prescribed by law."[5] Richardson was proposing that the so-called "reserves" become reserves in truth rather than in name only. When banks, in times of stress, reached the limits prescribed by law they would no longer have to resort to suspension, but could use the funds on hand to pay depositors. They would also be able to renew maturing loans, causing less disruption in domestic trade.

Although it had long been recognized that changes in the lending rate were a means of controlling outstanding credit,

5. Richardson in *Annual Report*, p. xviii.

the National Banking Act set 7 percent as the maximum interest rate which could be charged. Richardson apparently believed that in times of financial stress, banks should have some way to encourage liquidation without resorting to credit rationing.

The New York Clearing House Committee also noted these two problems. The committee felt that the reserves of country banks were too low and estimated that because of pyramiding, total reserves did "not finally much exceed ten percent of their direct liabilities, without reference to the large amount of debt which is otherwise dependent upon the same reserves." The committee therefore recommended that Congress give the Clearing House Committee "the power of deciding when the time or the emergency has arisen in which the public interest requires a relaxation of a rigid legal requirement in respect to the reserve of the banks in New York City." The committee also decried the usury laws which deprived the banks "of the power which is so effectively used by the principal banks of Europe, of protecting or augmenting their resources by adjusting the rate of interest to the necessities of the occasion—a power which, if practicable, Congress might safely confer upon the clearing house committee . . . with great advantage to the country."[6] Thus as early as 1873 the New York banks had recognized their importance as a stabilizing or destabilizing element under the provisions of the National Banking Act.

Of the three problems considered in this section, one was a question of bank practice and two were connected with the structure of the National Banking Act. The payment of interest on demand deposits was generally seen as a problem of bank practice, although others have viewed it as a structural flaw in the act. Without provisions allowing reserve pyramiding, this practice probably would not have caused much diffi-

6. See Sprague, *History of Crises*, p. 97.

culty. Nonetheless, the problem was considered amenable to solution by legislative action proscribing interest payments on demand deposits, and such action would most likely have been successful.

No action was taken regarding Secretary Richardson's recommendation on the use of reserves or the repeal of the usury law. Possibly many legislators felt banks would find some way to take advantage of such changes and use them to extend credit and increase profits, causing inflation and weakening their position. However, there can be little doubt that had Congress given the secretary of the treasury or the comptroller of the currency the power to suspend reserve requirements for a specified length of time without severe penalties, the impact of banking crises could have been lessened considerably, particularly if the usury laws also had been repealed. The banks would have been in a position to pay less attention to maintaining their reserves at a particular level and more attention to serving the public interest by maintaining the flow of commercial activities. At the same time they could have raised interest rates to encourage the liquidation of less profitable investments.

The first wave of reform proposals had little effect on the workings of the National Banking Act or on the banking philosophy upon which the act was secured. The proposals were not enacted nor were they in basic disagreement with prevailing banking philosophy. Indeed, basic principles were not really at issue during the National Banking era's early years; both the banking community and the general public were sanguine about banking's future under the National Banking Act. Given the banking practices which had typified the interregnum between the end of the Second Bank of the United States and the passage of the National Banking Act, this should not be too surprising.

The Move toward Asset Currency, 1893–1908

After the panic in 1893, there was a distinct change in the emphasis of reform proposals. The discussion shifted from banking practice to the alleged inelasticity of the national bank currency. This was a greater shift than might first be apparent.

By 1893 it became clear that under existing law substitution between the two major media of payment, checking deposits and notes, was often difficult. The soundness of the national bank notes was evidenced by depositors' willingness to accept them during panics. The soundness of the note issue was not questioned but rather the ability of the banks to redeem deposits.

To many, the culprit was the national bank currency's bond security. Critics maintained that any bond-secured currency was unresponsive to the needs of commerce. For that reason, banks sometimes were unable to satisfy customers when they wished to substitute currency for deposits; this lead to a crisis situation as the solvency of the banks was questioned. The proposed solution was a currency backed by all bank assets, but since most critics were bankers, they did not suggest the alternative of larger voluntary reserves.

Shortly after the crisis in 1873, Secretary Richardson recognized the glimmers of this line of thought when he remarked:

There is a prevailing sentiment that more elasticity should be given to the volume of the currency, so that the amount in circulation might increase and diminish according to the necessities of the business of the country. But the difference of opinion on this subject is so great, and the real difficulties attending to its solution are so numerous, that, without discussing any of the multitude of plans which have been presented to the public through the press and otherwise, I earnestly commend to the wisdom of Congress a careful and thorough consideration of this important subject, rendered more obviously important by the present embarrassed condition of large business interests which have suffered by the recent financial crisis.[7]

After 1893 the business and financial community was nearly unanimous in its desire to abolish bond-secured currency and issue a new national bank note secured by the assets of the issuing banks.

One of the first proposals to receive attention was presented at the American Bankers' Association annual convention in 1894 at Baltimore.[8] The location of the convention and the introduction of the plan by Baltimore bankers caused it to be commonly known as the Baltimore Plan. The plan's conception is generally credited to A. B. Hepburn, a New York banker; Horace White, editor of the *New York Evening Post*; and Charles G. Homer, a Baltimore banker.[9] The plan was presented to the convention by Homer and was discussed by Hepburn and White as if it had been conceived by a group of Baltimore bankers.[10] This procedure is an early indication of the subsequent approach of some New York bankers; fear of "Wall Street" was so great that they preferred to remain in the background.

The Baltimore Plan's provisions suggested the following amendments to the National Banking Act.[11] First of all, the provision requiring the deposit of bonds to secure circulation was to be repealed. Second, the plan argued for the establish-

7. Richardson in *Annual Report*, p. xvii.

8. This proposal has elsewhere been erroneously dated 1893. See Henry Parker Willis, *The Federal Reserve System* (New York: Ronald, 1923), p. 7; Redlich, *Molding of American Banking*, II, 210.

9. See Redlich, *Molding of American Banking*, II, 210.

10. *Proceedings of the American Bankers' Association Convention, 1894* (New York: American Bankers' Association, 1894), pp. 72–77, pp. 85–87.

sess., Vol. 1, Rept. 1126 (Washington: GPO, 1908).

ment of a new national circulation based on bank assets, amounting to three fourths of the banks' paid-up, unimpaired capital. The last third of this circulation was an "Emergency Circulation" and was subject to a heavy tax. The third major proposal was a "Guarantee Fund" for the circulation, presumably to ensure the soundness of the notes after the bond security was removed. The contributions made to the Guarantee Fund would have been used to redeem the notes of insolvent banks.

When he introduced the plan, Homer argued that American banks had historically maintained a circulation equal to about 40 or 50 percent of their capital, thus the plan would cause neither inflation or deflation. Hepburn used statistics to show that the Guarantee Fund provided more than adequate backing for the proposed note issue.[12] The plan's proponents felt that their proposal encompassed the best solution to the problem of inelasticity of the currency. The plan created a note issue which was adequate, given past experience, and an emergency currency would make it possible for banks to satisfy their depositors' demands when an abnormal amount of currency was desired.

The Baltimore Plan met with opposition, especially from some prominent New York bankers, and was never passed into law. However, it led to further consideration of extensive bank reform along credit currency lines both within the American Bankers' Association and in other groups of society. Within the association, proposals of this type continued to play an important role in all subsequent conventions. The debate culminated in the appointment of a currency commission by the association in 1906.

Other banking reform discussions were directly influenced by the Baltimore Plan. An example is that of the Indianapolis Monetary Convention of 1897, whose report was published in

12. Ibid., pp. 71, 74–75.

1898. Portions of the Indianapolis Plan were obviously influenced by the Baltimore Plan. While the convention primarily represented business interests, some bankers were also present, among them Charles G. Homer. The primary force behind the Monetary Commission selected at Indianapolis to draft a bill was J. Laurence Laughlin of the University of Chicago. Laughlin, from that time onward very active and influential in the reform movement, was charged with the preparation of the commission's final report. The report is very much a textbook on the history of banking and the theory of money.[13]

Some of the reforms proposed by the Indianapolis Monetary Commission in 1900 were much more far-reaching than those proposed by the American Bankers' Association in 1894, but the portions of the Monetary Commission's bill which dealt with banking reform were nearly identical to the Baltimore Plan. Under the Indianapolis Plan the bond backing for the note issue was to be eliminated over a ten-year period, and notes were then to be based on the assets of the issuing banks. A redemption fund and a guarantee fund were set up in the Monetary Commission Plan along lines similar to those in the Baltimore Plan. The main difference between the two plans was that the Indianapolis Monetary Commission Plan allowed banks to issue notes in an amount equal to their paid-up and unimpaired capital less the amount invested in real estate. However, the note issues above 60 percent of such capital were subject to an increasing tax.

The impact of the plans would have been similar. The potential note issue under the Monetary Commission Plan was larger, but the proponents of both plans believed that the

13. *Report of the Monetary Commission of the Indianapolis Convention of Boards of Trade, Chambers of Commerce, Commercial Clubs, and Other Similar Bodies of the United States* (Indianapolis: Hollenbeck, 1900).

normal note issue would be about 50 percent of bank capital and that note issues exceeding that amount would occur only under crisis conditions. The progressive tax was an attempt to insure that this would be true.

The Indianapolis Monetary Commission Plan, like the Baltimore Plan, was not passed into law, but the basic ideas behind the two bills were not lost. The concept of currency based on bank assets found a new champion in Charles N. Fowler, chairman of the Committee on Banking and Currency of the House of Representatives. The panic of 1907 provided dramatic evidence that fundamental banking reform was needed. Agreement on the shape reform should take or how far-reaching it should be did not exist. Fowler was convinced that the proper answer was embodied in a bill reported by his committee.[14] The bill was an extension and refinement of the ideas incorporated in the Baltimore Plan and the Indianapolis Monetary Commission Plan, that is, a replacement of national bank notes with notes backed by bank assets, and a guarantee fund provided by the banks. Fowler proposed the establishment of bank-note redemption districts, each with a central redemption center where the notes of all banks located in that district would be redeemed. There were to be a maximum of 20 redemption districts. On the whole, the bill was very similar to its predecessors, but the idea of regional redemption districts marked one of the first steps away from atomistic banking toward some sort of centralization.

The United States, Canada, and the Asset Currency Concept

All the plans in the previous section proposed a banking system similar in many respects to the Canadian banking

14. U.S. Congress, House, Report of Charles N. Fowler from the Committee on Banking and Currency, *House Reports*, 60th Cong., 1st sess., Vol. 1, Rept. 1126 (Washington: GPO, 1908).

system. In Canada bank notes depended directly on the assets of the banks. In 1890 Canadian banks themselves requested that a redemption and guarantee fund be added to the system. Connections between Canadian banks and American banks had always been close, especially in New York and areas where trade and general intercourse between the two countries existed, so that familiarity with Canadian practices is not surprising. Interest in the Canadian system was heightened by the stability and absence of bank failures which characterized the Canadian system.

While Canadian banking practice and theory may have influenced the three proposals discussed in this section, there is some question about the relevance of the Canadian experience to American banking. Canada had comparatively few banks; in 1900 there were fewer than forty banks in the whole country. Also, the Canadian banks were very large compared to those in the United States. The minimum capital for a Canadian bank was $500,000, but most had much more. The minimum capital for a national bank in the United States ranged from $50,000 to $200,000, depending upon the bank's location. In addition, branch banking enabled Canadian banks to spread their business over the entire country. This was not true of a "national" bank in the United States, where business was primarily concentrated in the bank's immediate vicinity and where branch banking was the exception rather than the rule. Note redemption was much easier in Canada, since a Canadian bank whose home office was in Quebec City had branches across the country where its notes could be redeemed. On the other hand, if a Chicago bank held the notes of a New York bank, they would have to be redeemed at the only office which the New York bank operated—the one in New York. In Canada notes eventually returned to the branch which issued them, but the transaction could be handled as an interbank transfer of funds.

Neither the Baltimore Plan nor the Indianapolis Monetary Commission Plan took into account the very real differences between Canadian and American banking practices, though both reports singled out the stability of the Canadian system as an example of the benefits of their plans. Either the differences were not realized or there was a belief that the differences were minor. One would suspect the former of the Baltimore Plan and the latter of the Indianapolis Monetary Commission Plan.

Proponents of the Fowler Bill recognized that the Canadian and American banking situations differed, particularly regarding redemption when each bank was allowed to issue its own notes. The Fowler Bill handled this problem by creating bank-note redemption districts. Notes would bear the number of the bank's redemption district, making it easier for banks to redeem "foreign" notes.

The most important consideration in adopting asset currency was a desire for banking stability. Few, if any, recognized that the Canadian system's stability was more likely the result of a few banks doing a widespread business than of the type of notes issued. A Canadian bank's business was nationwide, encompassing the whole economy. One bank might finance agriculture in the prairie provinces and industry in the East, giving great scope and stability to its investments—a diversified portfolio, so to speak. On the other hand, even though branch banking had been proposed for national banks, it is unlikely that any national bank would have had operations as diversified and therefore as free from large fluctuations as Canadian banks. There could have been grave implications if each bank was allowed to issue its own notes, especially in the case of smaller banks dealing almost entirely in one sector of the country's economy; a depression in that sector might seriously depreciate the value of the assets on which the notes were based. In fact, the major objection to all three proposals was that the atomistic banking structure of the United States lent a great deal of danger to a plan which allowed individual banks to issue notes on their assets. This same problem was to re-appear during the creation of the Federal Reserve System.[15]

Nevertheless, such drawbacks do not seem to have caused the rejection of these three proposals. It is difficult to say why the Baltimore Plan was rejected, although lack of popularity with the New York banking community alone made its adoption unlikely. The plan could not find a single supporter on the House Banking and Currency Committee and was never discussed. For the Indianapolis Monetary Commission Plan, however, some legislative result could have been expected. The Republican party's resistance to banking reform made it extremely difficult for any proposal to reach a vote in the whole House, especially a bill as far-reaching in impact as the Indianapolis Monetary Commission bill. Part of the bill eventually became the basis of the Gold Standard Act of 1900, but the bill's proposals for banking and currency reform never reached a vote.

While one can argue that the Baltimore Plan and the Indianapolis Monetary Commission bill were presented before their time, that cannot be said of the Fowler Bill. When the Fowler Bill was presented the national economy was recovering from the panic of 1907, amid a clamor for banking reform. Obviously some legislation was going to result, but that legislation was not to be the Fowler Bill.

The Fowler Bill and the Aldrich-Vreeland Act

About the same time that Representative Fowler introduced his plan, Senator Nelson Aldrich also proposed a bill designed to correct certain evils in the banking system. The two differed

15. See Chapter 10.

greatly. The Aldrich Bill of 1908 was an emergency currency bill. Instead of reforming the existing system, Aldrich proposed a system of currency associations organized by the banks themselves on a voluntary basis. In times of crisis these associations would issue emergency currency backed by bonds deposited by the banks. Federal, state, and local government bonds and railroad bonds were to be eligible as security for this emergency currency. Notes would be issued in an amount equal to 75 percent of the cash value of the bonds. Aldrich candidly admitted that it was his objective to create a national market for such bonds. The provisions of the Aldrich Bill drew much criticism, from western bankers in particular. The sort of assets eligible under the bill as security for emergency currency were not the sort that western banks generally carried in their portfolios. Opposition of another kind came from those who believed that the Aldrich Bill was nothing more than a scheme to aid the "Money Trust."[16]

Fowler's credit currency and Aldrich's bond-secured emergency currency were diametrically opposed. On the one hand Fowler's bill demonstrated a belief in the principle of commercial banking based on "quick" assets. Aldrich, however, by proposing a plan which would force the banks to invest in long-term securities, was taking a completely different view of the proper nature of bank assets. The final result was a compromise of a sort between the Fowler view and the Aldrich view— a compromise "of a sort" in that another bill was substituted for the Fowler Bill. The new bill, called the Vreeland Substitute, accepted asset currency but only as an emergency currency. The Vreeland emergency currency was based on commercial paper rather than on government or railroad bonds. The compromise, known as the Aldrich-Vreeland Act, simply

16. See Nathaniel Wright Stephenson, *Nelson W. Aldrich* (New York: Scribner's, 1930), chap. 20.

combined the two bills, creating currency associations which could issue heavily taxed emergency currency based on either commercial paper or certain specified types of long-term bonds. In the end, railroad bonds were not included as eligible security. Those who advocated a currency based on commercial paper at last had a foot in the door. The Aldrich-Vreeland Act also marked the first tendency for legislation to move toward some sort of centralization and cooperation among banks.

The Aldrich-Vreeland Act was never used in its original form. It was considered a temporary measure until more complete legislation could be drafted and passed. When the Federal Reserve Act was passed, the Aldrich-Vreeland Act was extended in an amended form. The extension allowed the nation to escape a possible critical situation on the eve of war in Europe. The long-term importance of the Aldrich-Vreeland Act was its creation of the National Monetary Commission, which was to study banking and money problems and propose solutions. This commission played an important role in banking reform.

Despite an earlier inclination to concentrate on bank practice, by 1908 two tendencies had emerged. The first was a movement toward asset currency and the second was a recognition of the need for cooperation, if not centralization. Both tendencies marked important departures from previous discussion; bond-secured currency and atomistic banking were no longer inviolable. The next step in the reform movement was to consolidate and expand on these gains.

CHAPTER 3

Paul M. Warburg and Victor Morawetz

The panic of 1907 is a convenient reference point for a discussion of banking reform. As we saw, the asset currency concept made its appearance in a relatively well-known proposal as early as 1894. However, this type of currency and the theory behind it were unable to supplant their arch-rivals—bond-secured currency and an emphasis on safety. Conditions changed considerably after 1907. Emergency currency based on commercial assets held by banks made its first legislative appearance in the Aldrich-Vreeland Act. Although the act provided that emergency currency could also be secured by certain specified long-term bonds, the Aldrich-Vreeland Act was bond-secured currency's last gasp. After 1908 the emphasis was on asset currency.

The asset currency concept did undergo some change, however. Earlier plans which incorporated the "asset" currency idea discussed notes backed by bank assets without regard to salability, time to maturity, and so forth. The new proposals were more definite about the proper sort of asset backing for bank notes: they specified short-term commercial bills. In a bona fide commercial banking system, there is no real difference between the early asset currency plans and the reform proposals made during the period from 1909 to 1912. But by 1909, writers realized that American bank assets often were not truly commercial, and to the extent that this was true, note issuing power should be curtailed.

Another important shift in the tenor of banking reform proposals occurred after 1907. Before then, even the most far-reaching plans had accepted the existing banking structure. The panic of 1907 convinced most people that control outside and above the banks was necessary. From control versus no control, the discussion shifted to the nature of the control to be instituted. The lines drawn have been common in American history—centralization versus decentralization.

The plans discussed in this chapter began to touch areas of wider significance. The revision of the asset currency concept and the increasing tendency toward central or regional control suggested new questions which lay beyond the elasticity problem. In general, these new matters involved credit rather than currency. Writers no longer addressed themselves exclusively to the establishment of mechanisms to allow easy convertibility between deposits and currency. A new concern had appeared, the determination of the aggregate money supply.

In spite of the advance, pre-1907 style proposals continued to appear. In 1909 the American Bankers' Association's Currency Commission proposed a plan which was little more than a restatement of the Baltimore Plan. The similarity is not surprising, since A. B. Hepburn was chairman of the Currency Commission. Representative Fowler also continued to espouse plans similar to his 1908 bill. Despite these remnants of the earlier period, the field was now open to plans which offered more radical changes in both the method and structure of American banking.

A nearly complete representation of this new trend can be found in the work of Paul M. Warburg and Victor Morawetz, both of New York. In their writings, Warburg and Morawetz provided the basic features of the Federal Reserve Act, although neither proposed or even accepted all the provisions later enacted into law.[1]

Paul M. Warburg

Paul Warburg was the single most powerful force in shaping the direction of American banking reform. Warburg himself claimed no originality, but through his writings, speeches, and counsel to those engaged in reform, he left an imprint greater than anyone else's. His influence has been denied by some who were unwilling to admit Warburg's importance for personal reasons but there were those who recognized his contribution. The economist E. R. A. Seligman was among those most lavish in praise. He maintained that Warburg changed the scope of banking reform and compared him to Samuel Jones Loyd, Lord Overstone, in his effects on banking law.[2]

In 1902, Warburg came to the United States to join Kuhn, Loeb and Company, one of the most respected and powerful banking houses in New York. Warburg's training and experience were gained in the family banking house in Hamburg, M. M. Warburg and Company, and his views had been shaped by his experience with European financial systems. Like most European bankers, Warburg viewed the American financial structure with a critical eye. Almost at once he began to suggest reform, an attitude which many American bankers no doubt found presumptuous. One New York banker's response to Warburg's suggestions probably demonstrated the typical

1. These two authors were not alone in proposing reform. Others were also active; Maurice Muhlman, for example, published a very detailed "Plan for a Central Bank" in *Banking Law Journal*, vols. 26 and 27, based, it would appear, on the Bank of England.

2. E. R. A. Seligman, Introduction to Paul M. Warburg, *Essays on Banking Reform in the United States by Paul M. Warburg, Proceedings of the Academy of Political Science*, 4 (July 1914), 387–390.

view of the existing financial system; James Stillman, powerful head of the National City Bank, was remembered by Warburg as believing that American banking methods represented an improvement upon the European system. According to Warburg, Stillman changed his view during the panic of 1907.[3]

Warburg's banking skills rapidly elevated him to a respected position in the New York banking community. Warburg continued to propose bank reform, often writing for leading journals and newspapers. In an article which first appeared in *The New York Times Annual Financial Review* early in 1907,[4] he lucidly described the defects in American practice and outlined remedies to help prevent panics such as the one shortly to occur.

Warburg strongly advocated the development of an American discount market and the European-style, two-name commercial paper necessary for the operation of such a market. For a banker of Warburg's background it was only a short step from a commercial bill market to a central bank. Warburg seems to have recognized very early that a full-fledged, European-style central bank was an impossibility in the United States. He realized that politics, not economic conditions, in the United States precluded the passage of any act which created a central bank. He always took care to indicate in his proposals the differences between what he proposed and a real central bank. His first reform proposal demonstrated this. Published at the very height of the 1907 panic, his essay was entitled "A Plan for a Modified Central Bank." This plan laid the groundwork for his later banking reform attempts and also gave the various asset currency plans a critical view. Warburg pointed out that the existing decentralization of reserves and

3. Paul Warburg, *The Federal Reserve System* (New York: Macmillan, 1930), I, 19.
4. Ibid., II, 9–25.

the proposed decentralization of the note issue would make it unlikely that stability could be ensured.

Warburg first met Nelson Aldrich in 1907. He quickly seized the opportunity to write Aldrich espousing his plan for a modified central bank. At the time Aldrich was cool toward the idea, and Warburg felt that he had made no progress.[5] He continued to write and speak, increasing both his contacts and the importance of his audiences. In 1908 he read a paper before the American Economic Association, and began to make contacts with leading economists which lasted for many years. While most economists seem to have supported some type of central bank, at least one well-known economist, O. M. W. Sprague of Harvard, did not. Warburg and Sprague had many exchanges during the next five years. Warburg attempted to answer Sprague's objections about the feasibility of modified central banking in the United States[6] and seems in the end to have achieved at least a partial conversion.[7] Warburg was the most effective advocate of reform along the lines of a central bank. He was able to argue convincingly that a properly restricted central bank was, if not the best reform, at least less objectionable than opponents had supposed.

The best statement of Warburg's ideas on reform can be found in two speeches he gave in 1910. One speech outlined the establishment of "A United Reserve Bank of the United States" and attempted to answer those who were skeptical about the feasibility of centralization. The second, entitled "Principles that Must Underlie Monetary Reform in the United States," further elaborated the principles underlying

5. Ibid., I, 31–32.
6. See O. M. W. Sprague, "The Proposal for a Central Bank in the United States: A Critical View," *Quarterly Journal of Economics*, 23 May 1909), 363–415.
7. See Warburg, *The Federal Reserve System*, I, 36.

the United Reserve Bank.[8] These two addresses took banking reform discussion to a new apex. Later reform plans made no theoretical advances on Warburg's 1910 proposals.

Warburg's second speech postulated four general principles:

(1) centralization of reserves;

(2) the establishment of commercial paper as a means of exchange between the central reservoir and the banks;

(3) fluidity of credit through the establishment of two-name commercial paper as the basis of the nation's banking assets;

(4) the creation through the central reservoir of an intercity clearinghouse to economize on cash remittances.

These ideas were not new or original, but they were presented in a form which was more acceptable than that of earlier proposals. They were clearly a reaction to the problems which had plagued American banking for the previous seventy years.

In his plan for a United Reserve Bank, Warburg proposed a bank located in Washington with a capital of $100 million, fully paid. The country would be divided into twenty operating zones similar to the currency association districts created under the Aldrich-Vreeland Act. The system was to be governed from Washington by a board of directors selected by three groups: the banking associations created by the act, the stockholders, and the government. The government directors would have included the secretary of the treasury, the comptroller of the currency, and the treasurer of the United States, along with others. The directors selected by the stockholders were to be merchants or manufacturers, not bank or trust company presidents. The tenure of all but the three ex officio members

8. Both of these speeches are reprinted in Warburg, *The Federal Reserve System*, II, 117–179, and *The Reform of the Currency, Proceedings of the Academy of Political Science*, 1 (Jan. 1911). Many of Warburg's works on banking reform prior to 1913 are reprinted in *Essays on Banking Reform . . . by Paul Warburg*, mentioned earlier.

was limited. This board selected the United Reserve Bank's operating officers, known as governors, who served as long as their actions were satisfactory.

Warburg suggested that the United Reserve Bank's share capital could be apportioned to the member banks or sold to the public. Maximum dividends on the stock were to be 4 percent. This was to ensure that it would not be profitable for any interest to gain control of the bank. Any profits above 4 percent went to the government. Warburg also suggested a provision which limited the total number of votes granted to any one stockholder.

Deposits in the United Reserve Bank were to be accepted from the government or the member banks and from no one else. No interest was to be paid on the deposits, and they could be counted as cash for reserve purposes by the banks and trust companies which held them. The United Reserve Bank was authorized to buy from banking association members commercial paper with a currency of no more than twenty-eight days. Such bills were eligible for purchase only if they had been issued more than thirty days before the date of purchase. This practice was to ensure that the bills would be real commercial bills and not merely drawn for accommodation. A bill with more than twenty-eight days to run could be purchased from a bank if the bank's local association endorsed it.

The United Reserve Bank was also to be empowered to purchase banker's acceptances (a commercial bill "accepted" or guaranteed by a bank) having not more than ninety days to run. Bills drawn on European banks or firms were to be allowed under the same provisions as domestic acceptances so that American banks could capture the large acceptance business based on American production which previously had gone to European banks. The United Reserve Bank was to be empowered to deal in bullion, to contract for advances in bullion, and to buy and sell bonds and United States Treasury notes. It was also authorized to issue circulating notes which were payable in gold on demand. These notes were to be secured by eligible commercial paper and a gold reserve amounting to at least one third of the outstanding notes. The United Reserve Bank was to be the only note issuer in the United States.

The United Reserve Bank was allowed to establish branches in the cities where banking associations maintained their head offices. The bank was empowered to request that commercial banks using its services keep with it a cash balance commensurate with their business. Warburg believed in centralization of reserves but seems to have been reluctant to require it; Warburg probably could not imagine bankers refusing so obvious a need.

The European influence on Warburg's plan is obvious and not surprising. The provisions of his plan are similar in many respects to those of the German Reichsbank. This is especially true of the note issue provision. German bank law at the time required the same percentage of gold and commercial paper as was proposed in the United Reserve Bank plan.

The European influence on Warburg is important in another respect; given his background, Warburg could conceive of no basis for the operation of a monetary system other than real commercial bills. His great influence helped further the acceptance of this attitude even though it was at variance with American business practices. Warburg advocated a change in American methods so that a large part of European central banking practice could be transfered to the United States.

Victor Morawetz

Victor Morawetz, another important figure in banking reform during this period, was a corporation counsel educated at Harvard Law School. His business activities were connected mainly with the railroad industry, but he was also a bank director and had connections with the Morgan interests. He was general counsel and chaired the executive committee of the Atchison, Topeka, and Santa Fe Railroad from 1896 to 1909, a period when he was writing on money and banking. Morawetz had also received a master's degree in economics from Columbia College in New York. Though trained as a lawyer (he published several legal texts), he seems to have been very interested in economic matters. He belonged to both the American Economic Association and the Academy of Political Science, two important forums of the banking reform movement during the years from 1908 to 1914.

This chapter focuses on two works by Morawetz: first, his book on the banking and currency question published in 1909, and second, his article contributed to the volume *The Reform of the Currency*, published by the Academy of Political Science in 1911.[9] Morawetz's writings are curious, for they combine excellent and sophisticated diagnosis with naive and often faulty prescription.

In the preface to his book, Morawetz stated that the work was "the result of an attempt to discuss briefly the principal questions that are likely to engage the attention of the National Monetary Commission."[10] The book's first twenty or so pages discuss the banking problem in the United States in a very sophisticated manner. Morawetz early realized what many other authors did not; specifically, the real problem facing the American banking system during times of stress was not a

9. Victor Morawetz, *The Banking and Currency Problem in the United States* (New York: North American Review Publishing Co., 1909); "The Banking and Currency Problem and Its Solution," *The Reform of the Currency*, Proceedings of the Academy of Political Science, 1 (Jan. 1911).

10. Morawetz, *The Banking and Currency Problem in the United States*, Preface.

currency shortage but rather a credit shortage. The problem was that the banks, in supplying a large increase in the demand for currency, were forced to strip themselves of reserves and therefore had to contract their outstanding debts. As Morawetz himself put it:

It is obvious, then, that our currency question is really a question of bank credits and bank reserves. The problem is, while preventing any unsafe expansion of credits or the issue of any unsafe currency, to find a way, (1) to avoid a depletion of bank reserves and the consequent large reduction of bank credits in times when lawful money is withdrawn to pay taxes and is locked up by the government, or when lawful money is largely withdrawn for use as a circulating medium to move the crops, or to be hoarded; and (2) to enable the banks, in times of great business activity, to expand their deposit liabilities and their loans and discounts, and also adequately to increase their reserves of lawful money.[11]

Given these conclusions, it is surprising that Morawetz became bogged down in a discussion of note issues, which he stressed in the bulk of his work.

Morawetz's proposal was in two parts. Since he did not believe that a central bank was feasible, he proposed a system of divisional reserve banks. He saw a similarity between such a plan and the creation of central reserve cities under the National Banking Act. He maintained that

this desirable result [centralization of reserves] has not been attained effectually under the National Bank Act, because the depositing banks have distributed their reserves among a large number of banks in reserve cities and in central reserve cities, and the banks receiving these deposits have failed to administer their affairs in such manner as to enable them at all times to furnish reserve money to the depositing banks.[12]

11. Ibid., pp. 11–12. Emphasis is in the original.
12. Ibid., pp. 85–86.

To remedy this situation, Morawetz suggested sectional reserve banks administered and controlled through stock ownership by the banks in each section.

The divisional reserve bank concept was innovative, but also incorporated earlier ideas. The stress on regional organization was common to many plans. The Fowler Bill, the Aldrich-Vreeland Act, and the United Reserve Bank all contained this feature; however, Morawetz made an important change. Where Warburg had proposed centralized reserves and control in the United Reserve Bank, Morawetz proposed that both reserves and control be decentralized. Banks would be required to deposit part of their reserves in the sectional reserve bank. These sectional banks were to furnish reserve money to the member banks by paying checks upon deposit accounts or by rediscounting commercial paper. The regional banks were required to keep ample reserves of lawful money, and their business was restricted to receiving deposits, purchasing high quality, short-term paper and rediscounting paper for the member institutions. Unfortunately, Morawetz turned away from this suggestion without developing it further to concentrate on the note issue problem.

Morawetz wanted to authorize the national banks to form an association which would issue notes backed by the joint credit of the banks. The association itself would have no capital and could not receive deposits. When banks with a total capital of $250 million became members, the association would become operative. Management was in the hands of a board elected by the banks, but no policy became effective until approved by the secretary of the treasury acting for the government. The comptroller of the currency would be an ex officio member of the managing board. Board members would be chosen on the basis of capital stock with one vote for every $25,000 worth of stock.

Banks in the association could take out and issue notes to the value of their capital. National bank notes already issued by the bank would be counted in the total note issue. The managing board, with the secretary of the treasury's approval, would have the power to regulate the total authorized note issue. A bank could not issue notes unless its capital was fully paid and unimpaired.

Every bank which took out notes would be required to deposit a note redemption fund with the association. The managing board and the secretary of the treasury would determine the percentage to be kept, but the percentage would never be less than 20 percent of the outstanding notes. The two major discretionary powers granted to the managing board (subject to the secretary of the treasury's approval) were the regulation of the total note issue and the determination of the reserve percentage in the redemption fund.

Morawetz anticipated that as the redemption fund percentage changed, the banks would increase or decrease their general reserves. It was here that he made a serious analytical error. Morawetz maintained that a note issue of $1,200,000,000 against a 50 percent reserve would have no greater effect on the money supply than a note issue of $631,578,947 with a 5 percent reserve.[13] There would be no difference in effect on currency, but there would be a difference in effect on the money supply (currency plus demand deposits). If the average reserve required against deposits is 25 percent, in the first case switching $600,000,000 of reserves from banking deposits to supporting note issues would require a contraction of $2,400,000,000 in deposits to gain $1,200,000,000 in notes.

13. Ibid., p. 93.

This is a *net decrease* of $1,200,000,000 in the money supply. The second case, requiring only $31,578,947 in reserves for a note issue of $631,578,947 results in a net increase of $505,-263, 159 in the money supply (minus $126,315,778 in deposits plus $631,578,947 in notes).

This problem, apparently unseen by Morawetz, was a major drawback to the scheme. To solve the problem, the substitution of one medium of exchange for another, the reserve requirement for note issues would have to be at most equal to that on deposits. Otherwise, banks would be unwilling to take out notes except under emergency conditions when they were needed to satisfy a demand for hand-to-hand currency. Morawetz, however, did not favor the establishment of an emergency currency.[14] The plan's minimum reserve against note issues was 20 percent, a figure which probably exceeded national bank average required reserves and was certainly higher than the average real reserves. Bankers would soon learn that as they issued notes they reduced their total capacity to grant loans and discounts, the problem with credit which Morawetz had already noted. As long as the note reserve percentage remained above the deposit reserve percentage, bankers would tend to expand assets using deposits rather than notes.

It is amazing that such an error escaped Morawetz, given his earlier analysis; however, his book is riddled with such inconsistencies. Early in the book Morawetz states that "people would not carry in their pockets any more currency than at present. On the other hand, wherever the currency in circulation exceeds the amount which the people want to carry in their pockets, or keep in their tills and cash boxes, or to hoard, this excess will be deposited in the banks and trust companies." Later he says, "Our own experience indicates the result that would follow were the power to issue additional notes to be

14. Ibid., pp. 57–61.

given to each of the seven thousand National Banks in the United States, free from central control. The result would be that, at all times, each bank, without regard to the general credit situation, would put out as many notes as practicable, and thus there would be injected into the currency a wholly unelastic—that is to say, non-contracting—issue of bank notes."[15]

Nevertheless, despite some analytic errors, Morawetz's proposed sectional reserve banks had a great impact on the reform discussion. He was the first to suggest this structural reform. In his later paper Morawetz suggested that the note issue and reserve functions both be placed in the sectional reserve banks. In addition, he proposed a central authority to coordinate the functioning of the system. With this idea, he anticipated the Federal Reserve Board.

Summary

Warburg's work turned out to be nicely congruent to the National Monetary Commission's work, discussed in Chapter 4. By presenting proposals, Warburg convinced many opponents that it was possible to transplant a hybrid central banking theory to American soil. For those who remained unconvinced, he presented a well-thought-out and concrete proposal for further discussion. His proposals reflected many years of European banking experience. Unfortunately, the suitability of this experience as a guide for American banking reform was not much discussed. Morawetz's work was crucial for at least one reason—the divisional reserve bank proposal. His curious book had many good points; most prominent among them was an excellent discussion of financial stringencies and their causes. But errors in reasoning and inconsistencies in the application of theory flawed his plan. He also showed an un-

15. Ibid., pp. 8, 52.

explained tendency to concentrate on the note issue question rather than on problems of reserves and credit. An important point about these two plans is that they were the last to be apolitical. After this period, banking reform became embroiled in politics. Subsequent proposals were placed in one political camp or another, generally depending on the degree of centralization which they contained. This division tended to become more and more inflexible as time passed.

Regarding note issues, Warburg and Morawetz agreed that short term commercial credit (plus specie) was the only proper backing for note issue, and that more centralization was necessary. Plans allowing all banks to issue notes were no longer considered. Instead, the tendency was toward some sort of central agency with the power to issue notes and to require member banks to centralize reserves. Once the idea of control had been taken this far, two new questions arose: first, whether there should be regionally central organizations or a central organization operating through branches; second, whether control should be private or public. Of the four possible permutations, any legislative proposal had to choose one.

CHAPTER 4

The Aldrich Bill

To the general public the Aldrich Bill of 1911 appeared to be the result of the investigations of the National Monetary Commission. Actually, as most members of the commission were aware, the bill was not a direct outcome of the investigations; this fact was stressed by many critics of the bill. The effects which the investigations had on Nelson Aldrich and other important politicians were more significant than any direct relationship between the bill and the commission. The investigations turned up little which was not already known by experts in banking, but some arguments took on an aura of legitimacy with which they had not been blessed prior to the commission's reports. Many people who had previously been indifferent or opposed to reform were converted by the investigations.

Reform activities were not confined to investigating banking conditions and proposing legislation; proponents of the Aldrich Bill also set in motion a chain of events which resulted in the establishment of the National Citizens' League, a body designed to carry the argument for banking reform to the public. The league drafted booklets for use by speakers and published works on banking reform. This organization underwent substantial change during its existence. Though the league was created to promote banking reform consistent with the Aldrich Bill, and its executive officer, J. Laurence Laughlin of the University of Chicago, was an effective agitator for reform in that direction, the Citizens' League eventually supported measures which were in opposition to some of the basic principles of the Aldrich Bill.

The National Monetary Commission

Few people expected that any substantial reform would originate with the National Monetary Commission; evidence exists that skepticism was warranted. The chairman, Senator Nelson Aldrich, had long been a defender of the status quo in banking. In the preface to the last edition of her husband's book on currency, Emily Eaton Hepburn related a statement made by her husband about Aldrich and the commission. Hepburn said that the purpose of the commission was to "sidetrack the [banking reform] matter. He [Aldrich] created this Commission knowing that all proposed legislation would be referred to it, and that the Commission would thereby obtain control of the situation."[1]

It is difficult to say what changed Aldrich's mind about the possibilities of banking reform. One of the main tasks of the commission was a trip to Europe to interview European bankers. Aldrich asked Professor A. Piatt Andrew to bring along elementary books on money and banking. During the voyage, Andrew held classes for those members who were not well informed. Certainly if Aldrich's intention was to sidetrack monetary reform, it was not in his interest to educate the other members. The evidence indicates an explanation of Aldrich's behavior which is consistent with both sides of the story; Aldrich may really have believed in the theory behind bond-secured currency and felt that the evidence would support his belief. No other explanation adequately covers his intention to sidetrack further reform and his amazement when the testi-

1. A. Barton Hepburn, *A History of Currency in the United States,* rev. ed. (New York: Macmillan, 1924), pp. vii–viii.

mony of German bankers finally convinced him to desert his support for bond-secured note issues. The European bank interviews were only part of what was accomplished in Europe, for there was another convert to the gospel of banking reform.

In addition to the European trip, the commission published many American works on banking and arranged for others to be translated from German and French. The result was a wide-ranging portrait of American banking and bank practice as well as a large compilation of material on foreign banking.

Although it was nominally bipartisan, the National Monetary Commission became so identified with Nelson Aldrich that its very existence became a political issue. It was accused of having wasted government funds, and since the commission's investigations did not quickly give rise to a reform bill in Congress, it was charged that the commission was a failure. After debate, which was often vitriolic, a bill dissolving the commission was passed late in 1911.

The Cast of Characters

The bill finally approved by the National Monetary Commission, commonly known as the Aldrich Bill, was the first banking reform bill to receive widespread attention since the National Banking Act. The bill served notice that there were those in positions of importance who had resolved to reform American banking practice. The Aldrich Bill, though not directly considered in Congress because of political reasons, formed the legislative base of the Federal Reserve Act.

Given Aldrich's previous views, there was no less likely proponent of the Aldrich Bill than Senator Aldrich himself. Before the National Monetary Commission's voyage to Europe and the interviews which the commission obtained there with leading central and private bankers, Aldrich had not believed in any thorough banking reform. He instead favored legislation allowing national banks to issue currency backed by certain specified bonds in times of emergency. The European trip profoundly affected Aldrich, and he deserted the concept of bond-secured currency in favor of the plan embodied in the Aldrich Bill.

According to Nathaniel Wright Stephenson, Aldrich's biographer, the senator had definite ideas in mind when he composed the National Monetary Commission.[2] A small group of men made up the working body of the commission, with the others serving only as window dressing. Three men who were not officially on the commission had a major impact on the investigation. Aldrich asked J. P. Morgan, a personal acquaintance, to recommend a practical banking expert, and Morgan suggested Henry P. Davison, a Morgan partner. The commission's academic member was Assistant Professor A. Piatt Andrew of Harvard University, who was recommended by the president of Harvard, Charles William Eliot. Andrew later became Aldrich's personal economic adviser and a publicist for the Aldrich Bill. George M. Reynolds of Chicago, president of the American Bankers' Association, also was involved in the investigation.

It was during the commission's interviews with German bankers that Senator Aldrich had his revelation.[3] The account of the method used in Germany to meet currency requirements converted Aldrich to a belief in currency based on commercial assets: the conversion was both sudden and total. Upon his return to the United States, Aldrich astounded Paul Warburg with his new-found enthusiasm for central banking with an asset-backed currency.[4]

2. Stephenson, *Nelson W. Aldrich*, pp. 334–335.
3. Ibid., p. 339.
4. Ibid., p. 340, and Warburg, *The Federal Reserve System*, I, 56–57.

Nearly two years elapsed between the National Monetary Commission's return from Europe and any attempt to draft a bill. Even then it was not clear who suggested that a bill be drafted. Thomas W. Lamont, Davison's biographer, gives the impression that it was Davison who proposed a meeting.[5] Regardless of whose idea it was, the meeting took place in November of 1910 at Jekyll Island, Georgia. Secrecy surrounded the meeting, and the particulars seem not to have surfaced until 1930. Jekyll Island was a duck-shooting retreat for wealthy men. None of those present at the meeting were members, so one assumes that a member arranged for them to use the facilities; that member was most likely J. P. Morgan. While Morgan was not present at the meeting, he certainly had an interest in the proceedings. If the meeting actually was Davison's idea, it is even more likely that the arrangements were made by Morgan, since he and Davison were close associates. Though some news reporters found out about the gathering, secrecy was still maintained. According to Stephenson, Davison talked to the reporters and convinced them that there should be no publicity.[6] This request seems to have been honored, since the particulars of the meeting and even the names of those present were not known until 1930, when the authorized Aldrich biography was published.

The cast of characters at Jekyll Island differed slightly from that of the National Monetary Commission's European inquiry. Reynolds was not present, and Aldrich, Davison, and Andrew were joined by Paul Warburg and Frank A. Vanderlip, vice-president of the National City Bank of New York. Vanderlip, as well as Warburg, had been an early advocate of banking re-

5. Thomas W. Lamont, *Henry P. Davidson* (New York: Harper, 1933), pp. 96–97.
6. Stephenson, *Nelson W. Aldrich*, pp. 373–379, and Lamont, *Henry P. Davison*, pp. 96–101.

form. The two were kindred spirits who formed an important minority among New York bankers.

Those present at Jekyll Island—three bankers, one academician, and a politician—made up the group which forged a reform bill out of the National Monetary Commission's research. The group presumably included people grounded in practice, theory, and political realities. The bankers, especially Warburg, seemed less inclined than Aldrich to believe that the country would accept far-reaching reform, the politician Aldrich chided Warburg for being too timid about his proposals for banking reform.[7] Aldrich favored the idea of a central bank based on the European model, while Warburg, and likely the others as well, favored a modified central bank. On this question, Warburg and his colleagues were probably better attuned to public sentiment.

Specifics

The Jekyll Island plan was modified after its initial presentation to the National Monetary Commission, but the plan was not changed in any substantial way. Some parts were rewritten for easier interpretation and to conform to common construction, but most essential features remained the same.

The Aldrich Bill's basic features were the same as those in Paul Warburg's United Reserve Bank plan,[8] published in March 1910 about eight months before the Jekyll Island meeting. The Aldrich Bill proposed the establishment of a National Reserve Association with a paid-in capital stock of at least $100 million, wholly owned by subscribing banks. The head office was to be in Washington, D.C., with fifteen branches. Each of the fifteen districts was to be divided into local associations of

7. Stephenson, *Nelson W. Aldrich*, p. 340, and Warburg, *The Federal Reserve System*, I, 56.
8. See Chapter 3.

at least ten banks. These local associations were to join together to select the board of directors for the district as well as a board for themselves. On the local level, three fifths of the directors were to be chosen by the banks, but the remainder on the basis of stock ownership. At the district level, one half were to be chosen by the banks, one third on the basis of stock ownership, and one sixth were to be selected by the other directors.

There were three remarkable aspects of this plan: first, no provision was made for the public or the government to hold stock in the National Reserve Association, though Warburg's original plan had suggested that the public might be allowed to hold some stock; second, an attempt was made to provide more representation for smaller banks than would have been provided by an election process based on stock ownership; third, the whole organizational structure obviously was based on the clearinghouse principle which had aided many cities, especially New York, in overcoming financial panics. Aldrich freely acknowledged this last fact in the speeches he made supporting his bill, and three of the bankers in the group, particularly Davison, had seen the benefits of the clearinghouse method firsthand; clearly they decided to stress the bill's familiar aspects rather than the changes it represented. In a speech given before the American Bankers' Association's annual convention in 1911, Aldrich said, "The organization proposed is not a bank, but a *cooperative union* of all the banks of the country for definite purposes and with very limited and clearly defined functions. It is, in effect, an extension, an *evolution of the clearing-house plan* modified to meet the needs and requirements of an entire people."[9]

9. *Address of Nelson W. Aldrich, Chairman of the National Monetary Commission, Before the Annual Convention of the American Bankers' Association at New Orleans, Tuesday, November 12,*

The board of directors of the National Reserve Association was chosen as follows: two directors chosen by each district, one of them to represent agricultural, commercial, industrial, and other interests of the country; nine directors chosen on the basis of stock ownership with no more than one director from any district; and seven ex officio members—a governor, to be chairman of the board, two deputy governors, and the secretary of the treasury, the secretary of commerce and labor, the secretary of agriculture, and the comptroller of the currency. The governor was to be selected by the president from a list presented by the elected board, and could be removed for cause by a two thirds vote of the board. The deputy governors were elected by the board and could be removed and replaced for cause by a majority vote of the board at any time. All elected members were to serve three-year terms. The bill also provided for an executive committee which probably would have been the association's working body. This committee was to have nine members, five of whom would have been selected from the board. The other members were to have been the governor, who was ex officio chairman, the two deputy governors, and the comptroller of the currency.

An important structural feature of the national board of directors is the lack of government participation. Of forty-six directors, only six were appointed by the president, and one of those from a list given him by the board. On the executive board, the government members were outnumbered five to four. This aspect of the plan apparently was favored by Aldrich and Davison and opposed by Warburg, who felt that the government should have more influence. However, the difference

---

1911 (Washington, 1911), reprinted in Herman E. Kroos and Paul Samuelson, *Documentary History of Banking and Currency in the United States* (New York: Chelsea House, 1969), III, 1202. Emphasis is in the original.

of opinion probably was not great, since in Warburg's United Reserve Bank plan only one fifth of the directors represented the government. Later, Warburg favored majority government control of the reserve system.[10]

The government's influence in choosing the board of directors was to become an important topic. In fact, one of the most important changes made in the bill from the first draft to the second concerned the board's power to remove the governor. The original bill gave this power to the president; however, that provision was unacceptable to the American Bankers' Association Currency Committee, and Aldrich changed the plan to acquire their support.[11]

The question of membership was left up to the individual banks; any national banking association could join without making any changes in its operation. State banks and trust companies were also eligible for membership, but they were required to meet conditions on capital and reserves similar to those set out in the National Banking Act. This provision ensured that these banks would not have a competitive advantage over national banks. The only method by which a subscribing bank could leave the association was liquidation.

Each bank was to subscribe to an amount of stock equal to 10 percent of its paid-in, unimpaired capital. Fifty percent of the subscription was to be paid on joining the association. The amount of capital stock in the National Reserve Association held by a bank was to increase and decrease in proportion to any increase or decrease in its own capital. In this way, the capital of the entire association would increase and decrease. The stockholders could receive a maximum 5 percent return with the rest going into a surplus fund or to the United States as a franchise tax. This limitation of payments to stockholders

10. Warburg, The Federal Reserve System, I, 90–91.
11. Stephenson, Nelson W. Aldrich, pp. 389–394.

was considered essential by Warburg and others who saw it as an assurance to the general public that an attempt by Wall Street or others to gain control of the National Reserve Association would not be a profitable venture. The association could therefore operate as a quasi-public institution which would be responsive to the public interest. This provision, along with the election procedure, probably was viewed as sufficient justification for the dominance of bankers and businessmen on the boards of directors. The authors felt that bankers and businessmen were the only persons qualified to run such an organization, but they wanted to eliminate public fear that the system would be captured by Wall Street.

The National Reserve Association was not a central bank of the European kind. It was allowed to deal with the government or subscribing banks only, except in purchases and sales of federal, state, or foreign government securities, and gold coin or bullion. The association was not allowed to pay interest on any deposits.

The National Reserve Association's rediscount functions were to be handled through the branches. Notes and bills of exchange, endorsed by a member bank, would be rediscounted if they represented agricultural, industrial, or commercial transactions, but not if they were drawn to carry stocks, bonds, or other investment securities. Notes presented to the association for discount were to have a maturity of not more than twenty-eight days and were to have been made at least thirty days prior to the date of rediscount. Such a provision was intended to ensure that all rediscounted notes represented commercial, industrial, or agricultural transactions; the discount provisions of the proposed statute were a clear attempt to legislate the real bills doctrine.

Banks could rediscount bills with more than twenty-eight days to run only if they were guaranteed by the member bank's local association. It was felt that the local associations could best determine the nature and soundness of longer-term bills. Banks had to pay for the guarantee, and in no case were the bills to run longer than four months. The discounting sections of the Aldrich Bill very closely resembled those in Warburg's United Reserve Bank plan.

Under certain conditions, the National Reserve Association would be allowed to discount a member bank's direct obligations. Such obligations would have to be secured, and the discount would be limited to 75 percent of the value of the securities pledged. The discount rate at which all discount and rediscount transactions were to take place was to be set by the board of the National Reserve Association. The rate was to have been uniform throughout the United States.

The National Reserve Association was empowered to purchase bankers' acceptances of the kind known as "prime bills," bills drawn by well-known companies, and two-name foreign drafts or bills of exchange, with ninety days or less to run, but from member banks only. They were also allowed to purchase all federal government securities, and state and foreign government securities with maturities of one year or less. The National Reserve Association was empowered to deal in gold coins and bullion, to make loans upon and to borrow gold coins and bullion giving acceptable security. The association was also given the power to establish banking agencies in foreign countries and to hold deposits in foreign banks to carry out its overseas activities.

Since state banks and trust companies were to be allowed to join the National Reserve Association, national banks were to be allowed to expand their operations into areas where state banks operated but national banks were forbidden. The Aldrich Bill authorized national banks to accept bills or drafts drawn on them if those notes had no more than four months to run, were properly secured, and represented the same type of commercial transactions as other eligible bills. The acceptances of any bank were limited to one half the bank's capital and surplus. National banks were also authorized to loan up to 30 percent of their time deposits on improved and unencumbered real estate, but banks acting as reserve depositories for other banks were not allowed this privilege.

The reserve percentages of the member banks were not to be changed from those required by the National Banking Act. For thirty days before the maturation of time deposits, reserve requirements were set at the same levels as for demand deposits, but no reserves were to be required before that date. The Aldrich Bill made no provision concerning the location of reserves, so the prevailing structure of reserves would have remained legal; deposits in the association's branches would have qualified as reserves, as would the notes of the association.

The association was to take over responsibility for the redemption of national bank notes; the intention was to substitute the National Reserve Association's notes for national bank notes. The National Reserve Association's demand liabilities, both deposits and notes, were to be covered by a 50 percent reserve of gold or other lawful money of the United States. A tax was assessed on any deficiency, and the tax increased by one percent for every 2 1/2 percent that the reserve fell below 50 percent. In no case could note issues increase after the gold reserve had reached 33 1/3 percent. In computing the demand liabilities, a sum equal to one half of the bonds purchased by the association from the national banks was to be deducted. The 50 percent reserve applied only to the issue below $900 million. All notes above that amount were to be backed by an equal amount of lawful money or subject to a graduated tax. The notes were to have been legal tender for all government dues (except those specifically payable in gold), and for all transactions between financial institutions.

The Aldrich Bill allowed for the organization of banking companies to do business in foreign countries. Minimum levels of capital were set, and the foreign banking companies were forbidden to engage in deposit banking inside the United States. The intent of this provision was to expand the scope of foreign trade financing, since many people in the financial world felt that American banks had not been getting a fair share of international banking trade.

The Aldrich Bill was by far the most comprehensive reform plan to appear before the Federal Reserve Act. With the exception of the organizational aspects, the provisions of the bill were adopted almost verbatim into the Federal Reserve Act. Even though most portions of the Aldrich Bill were eventually accepted, in 1912 the bill did not meet with general acceptance. Its association with Nelson Aldrich created suspicion in many quarters, particularly in the Democratic party; other sectors of the country, which identified the bill with the banking community were equally wary. At the time the Aldrich Bill was being prepared, its proponents realized that it would be controversial, so they decided that a nationwide educational campaign was desirable, and created the National Citizens' League.

The National Citizens' League

The National Citizens' League grew out of a resolution proposed at the meetings of the National Board of Trade in January 1910 by the ubiquitous Paul Warburg. The resolution suggested that January 18, 1911, be set aside as a "monetary day" to be devoted to a "Business Men's Monetary Conference." At that conference a committee of seven, with Warburg as chairman, was appointed to organize a businessmen's monetary reform league.[12] The committee met in Chicago on April 26, 1911. Some of the leading men in Chicago, including John G. Shedd, Harry A. Wheeler, Cyrus McCormick, Charles H. Wacker, Frederic A. Delano, J. Laurence Laughlin, John V. Farwell, and Fred W. Upham, were persuaded to oversee the formation of the "National Citizens' League, the object of which shall be to give organized expression to the growing public sentiment in favor of, and to aid in, securing the legislation necessary to insure an improved banking system for the United States of America."[13]

The choice of Chicago as the league's home was clearly a political move. An effective propaganda campaign meant that it was necessary for the league not to be associated in the public mind with New York or Wall Street. The league's elected officials were from the midwest in order that the well-known New York banking figures, Warburg, Vanderlip, Davison, Aldrich, and others, would not be formally associated with the league. The president was John V. Farwell of Chicago and the chairman of the league's executive committee was J. Laurence Laughlin of the University of Chicago, who was the league's active head and the editor of its publications. Laughlin had drafted the *Report of the Indianapolis Monetary Commission* and wrote a pamphlet entitled *Suggestions for Banking Reform*, setting out the chief principles of banking reform, and was a well-known expert on monetary affairs. The league's main output, a volume titled *Banking Reform*, was written by Laughlin and H. Parker Willis. Willis had been Laughlin's student at the University of Chicago, and his assistant in the preparation of the *Report of the Indianapolis Monetary Commission*.

12. See J. Laurence Laughlin, ed., *Banking Reform* (Chicago: Blakely Printing Company, 1912), p. 419, and Warburg, *The Federal Reserve System*, I, 68, 582–584.

13. Laughlin, ed., *Banking Reform*, p. 420.

While there is little doubt that Warburg's original intention was to create a body to promote the Aldrich Plan, the league never advocated any particular plan, and concentrated instead on promoting general principles. The league's statement of purpose was as follows:

(1) Cooperation, not dominant centralization, of all banks by an evolution out of our clearing house experience
(2) Protection of the credit system of the country from the domination of any group of financial or political interests
(3) Independence of the individual banks, national and state, and uniform treatment in discounts and rates to all banks, large or small
(4) Provision for making liquid the sound commercial paper of all the banks, either in the form of credits or bank notes redeemable in gold or lawful money
(5) Elasticity of currency and credit in times of seasonal demands and stringencies, with full protection against over-expansion
(6) Legalization of acceptances, or time bills of exchange, in order to create a discount market at home and abroad
(7) The organization of better banking facilities with other countries to aid in the extension of our foreign trade.[14]

Although this is a very general set of principles, they obviously were derived from the Aldrich Bill, and also bear a strong resemblance to Warburg's "Principles which Must Underlie Monetary Reform." The emphasis on clearinghouses, a uniform discount rate, and the avoidance of political domination make up integral parts of the Aldrich Bill, and are repeatedly used as examples of desirable change in the volume *Banking Reform*. In Laughlin's pamphlet, *Suggestions for Banking Reform*, he did not directly support the Aldrich Bill, but left no doubt that the bill contained many or all of the necessary ingredients for banking and monetary reform.

When Willis wrote his monumental work on the Federal

14. Ibid.

Reserve System, he chose to ignore the role which he and Laughlin had played in the propaganda of the National Citizens' League. Willis maintained that the league was the propaganda organ of the banking community.[15] His statement was probably true, but the league spoke with the voice of Laughlin and Willis, both of whom—especially Willis—were later to be arrayed against the Aldrich Bill.

The National Citizens' League probably accomplished its task. It created popular acceptance of the need for banking reform and ensured that it would proceed along the general lines of the Aldrich Plan. The movement grew until some action was inevitable. That action was not the passage of the Aldrich Bill, but of something very similar.

Prospects

Two important questions arise concerning the Aldrich Bill: whether or not its provisions would have succeeded in dealing with the problems they proposed to solve; and why the bill was not accepted.

Clearly, much of the Aldrich Bill was influenced by a particular line of banking and monetary thought: the real bills doctrine. The bill was not criticized on this account, though portions of it which involved propositions separate from the real bills theory were criticized. Primarily the criticism centered on the reserve provisions, especially on the location of reserves and what sort of assets were eligible to be counted as reserves. The uniform rate of discount was also hotly debated. There were other controversial provisions, such as the discount of domestic acceptances and a member bank's direct obligations. The question of organization was far from settled, and this plagued the Aldrich Bill endlessly. If one factor was criti-

15. Willis, *The Federal Reserve System*, pp. 149–150.

cal to the bill's failure, it was the type of control contained in the proposal.

The Aldrich Bill's reserve provisions and the discussion surrounding them are curious in many ways. The point most often stressed by Aldrich and Warburg was the necessity of cooperation in the use of reserves. It was generally agreed that the best way to accomplish such cooperation was to place reserves in a central reservoir, hence the name National Reserve Association. By 1907 it was apparent to all that the National Banking Act's reserve provisions did not allow reserves to be used properly; instead of functioning as a contingency fund for emergencies, bank reserves were locked up by the law.[16]

The obvious solution to the problem was a centralization of reserves to replace the pyramiding which developed under the National Banking Act; a central organization could react swiftly to alleviate pressure where it occurred. Warburg often used the metaphor of a central water reservoir with which a city could protect itself against fire, versus the distribution of water among the many property owners. Aside from allowing deposits held with the National Reserve Association to be counted as reserves, the Aldrich Bill did not change the National Banking Act's reserve structure at all. Perhaps Aldrich, Warburg, and others felt that the need to centralize reserves was obvious; legislation on the matter needed only to create a reservoir, and the banks would fill it out of their own self-interest.

Since the National Reserve Association would not have been allowed to pay interest on any of its deposits, and national banks could have continued to pay interest on their deposits, any bank which transferred all its reserves to the National Reserve Association would reduce its total profits. If banks kept balances with the National Reserve Association in

16. See Chapter 1.

amounts necessary only to facilitate clearings, the central reservoir might not have been large enough to be effective.

Another important issue was whether or not member banks should be allowed to count the association's notes as reserves when those notes were held in their own vaults. The original Aldrich Plan drafted at Jekyl Island prohibited this practice because Aldrich himself was against it, though Warburg favored it. When the National Monetary Commission met with the American Bankers' Association Currency Committee, the latter requested—some say demanded—that banks be allowed to count the notes they held as reserves.[17]

At the same time, the book published by the National Citizens' League argued against such a practice and attempted to present a theoretical argument against it. Briefly, the argument was that banks could discount bills, receive notes, and place the proceeds in their reserves allowing a multiple expansion of credit. However, if notes were not taken as the proceeds of the discount and the money was left as a deposit in the National Reserve Association, it could be the basis of an equal expansion of credit. In another case, a bank which received payment in notes of the Reserve Association could either keep the notes in its own vault, using them as reserves, or send them to the National Reserve Association where its reserve account would be increased; either way, the reserves of such a bank would remain the same.[18]

There are two main reasons why the authors became confused. First, they wished to ensure that notes were returned to the association when they were no longer needed for circulation. This idea was a carry-over from the debate on elasticity and was a result of their view of the real bills doctrine. Laughlin later drew up a reform plan of his own which he sent

17. Stephenson, *Nelson W. Aldrich*, pp. 389–394.
18. Compare Laughlin, ed., *Banking Reform*, pp. 157–159.

to Willis when the latter became the expert for the House Committee on Banking and Currency. Laughlin's plan will be discussed later; however, in this context one might point out that his plan would have allowed neither the notes of his proposed system nor the deposits arising from rediscounts to be counted as reserves. An extension of this would be to prohibit member banks from counting as reserves the notes they received during the normal course of business, and then sent to the reserve organization, because the member bank might be merely depositing an excess of till money. Since the bank could get no credit by sending the notes on to be used as reserves, it would be likely to reissue the notes as loans. The practice is exactly what Laughlin wanted to prevent.

Few of the period's major writers, certainly not Willis or Laughlin, seemed to understand the way a centralized fractional banking system really worked, particularly regarding credit and its effects on aggregate demand. Their basic problem was an inability to conceptualize the notion of "high-powered money." Many practical bankers—Warburg is the best example—though never explicitly acknowledging this concept, demonstrated that they understood how it worked. Many times Warburg asserted that all the debts of a central bank had the same characteristics, whether they were notes in the hands of the member banks or deposits at the reserve institution. Willis and Laughlin were not able to move beyond the acknowledged fact that national banks should be prevented from counting their notes as reserves; national banks could not be allowed to create their own reserve money without any outside limitations. This argument does not hold, however, once a central reservoir is created. If one type of central organization debt is eligible for use as reserves and all types are interchangeable, it is nonsensical to make any single type ineligible for use as reserves.

These debates demonstrate the problems encountered in drafting a reform bill. Pleasing everyone and creating a bill which was internally consistent was a difficult proposition. The two reserve questions discussed here are good examples. The fact that the reserve structure was not completely reformed by the Aldrich Bill was unfortunate. Allowing member banks to count the notes of the National Reserve Association as part of their reserves demonstrated a relatively sophisticated understanding of banking. On general matters concerning discounts agreement had been reached and only various problems with reserves and a few other matters remained to be sorted out. The question of control, for instance, was still very much undecided. Both aspects of control were still being debated—public versus private and centralized versus decentralized.

The Aldrich Bill stood foursquare for private control; Aldrich's conservatism would not allow the possibility of government control, and the National Reserve Association's administration was put in the hands of the member banks. A complicated election procedure had been devised to limit the influence of larger banks, no doubt in response to the widespread and expanding fear of the "Money Trust."

The intricate election procedure was only one of several attempts to allay this fear. When any one person, partnership, or corporation owned 40 percent or more of the stock in each of two or more banks, the bill regarded that owner as a unit with only one vote. Furthermore, the rate of return on capital was limited to diminish the profitability of controlling the system. Control of discount rates and influence over bank policy held out possibilities of gain far greater than any to be obtained from simple dividend payments, but this matter was overlooked. At any rate, the probability of high returns from such manipulations was small, if the National Reserve Association was operated in the public interest.

One reason for placing control in the hands of bankers was that in Europe the government had little or nothing to do with the day-to-day operation of most central banks, and there was nothing to indicate that the United States government was any more qualified in this regard than European governments. On the other hand, the average American banker, especially the smaller country banker, had not demonstrated any extraordinary capacity or inclination to serve the public interest, since poor banking practices had been widespread throughout the United States. The bankers who had demonstrated the ability to view the larger picture and formulate plans to relieve the pressure caused by panics were the very bankers who were feared most by the general public—the Wall Street bankers. This fact can be seen again and again. The clearness of Warburg's conception of banking theory compared to that of Willis and Laughlin is a good example. The practical experience of bankers such as Paul Warburg, J. P. Morgan, Benjamin Strong, and others yielded the most advanced theory. When their advice was ignored or their policies overruled, the passage of time generally proved them correct. Anyone drafting a bill with a central organization to accomplish financial reform faced this problem: the groups whose support was needed to pass the legislation did not trust the people who were qualified to operate the system. In the end, the solution was government control of appointments with bankers as the appointees.

The control provisions of the Aldrich Bill reveal the banking community's influence; as presented to Congress the bill allowed the board, by a two thirds vote, to remove the governor for cause, but the original bill had provided for his removal by the president. The American Bankers' Association refused to accept the first version. Aldrich, believing that their support was essential, capitulated. The new provision was opposed by the Democratic party and probably would have met widespread resistance if the bill had been passed into law.

Another problem the Aldrich Bill faced was the National Reserve Association's centralized administration. Though the National Citizens' League and Aldrich's speaking tour had created some support for the idea of a centralized organization, the Democratic party was diametrically opposed to such a structure, and favored the divisional reserve bank system which Morawetz had proposed.

The tradition of the Democratic party was counter to centralized control, but its resistance to control may have been based on politics as much as on theory. It is very difficult to find evidence that Democratic party leaders had anything specific in mind except resistance to the Aldrich Bill when it was presented. They determined in 1912 to find a substitute.

CHAPTER 5

The Development of the Glass Bill

Just as the National Monetary Commission made its final report and presented its bill to Congress, the political environment changed substantially. The Democratic party gained control of the House of Representatives in 1910, and the Seventeenth Amendment to the Constitution caused an upheaval in the Republican-dominated Senate. There was also an ideological split among the Republicans themselves. Under these political conditions, the Aldrich Bill could make no headway whatsoever; the course of monetary and banking reform was in doubt.

This chapter covers the first part of the Federal Reserve Act's journey through Congress, and traces banking reform from the Democratic party's rise to power, through the passage of the Glass Bill by the House of Representatives. The process was profoundly affected by the political environment and the personalities involved. This was particularly true regarding questions of organization. While theoretical matters seemed settled, the same could not be said about organizational issues. The path of banking reform through Congress was repeatedly obstructed by the debate over the acceptable degree of centralization. As banking reform became enmeshed in politics, economic considerations were often pushed into the background.

Wilson, Glass, and Willis: The Glass Bill Takes Shape

In 1912 the Democrats gained control of both houses of Congress and Woodrow Wilson was elected president. The Democratic platform included a plank placing the party squarely against the Aldrich Bill. Many Democrats believed that the platform also placed them against any banking reform proposal with centralized organization. Since the position of some influential Democrats was unknown when it came to the banking question, there was much uncertainty. Woodrow Wilson had sidestepped the banking question during his campaign, preferring to speak in generalities without committing himself to any proposal. The chairman of the House Committee on Banking and Currency was retiring, and the ideas of the man second in seniority, Carter Glass, were little known. However, Wilson and Glass, between them, intended to take rapid action on the matter.

Both men had a limited familiarity with banking. Glass had gained some knowledge from his previous experience on the Banking and Currency Committee, but he was a newspaperman rather than a businessman or banker. He has been described by Paul Warburg as lacking the business mind possessed by Nelson Aldrich.[1]

Woodrow Wilson often has been portrayed as almost totally ignorant of banking details. He may in fact have been ignorant of details, but from the accounts given by Glass, Warburg, and Willis, he was knowledgeable about banking theory. He had taught economics at Princeton and was familiar with the works of William Stanley Jevons and Walter Bagehot.[2] Wilson may have been one of the few men outside university economics departments who was acquainted with Jevons's works on money; these works have never been given

1. Warburg, *The Federal Reserve System,* I, 58.
2. William Diamond, *The Economic Thought of Woodrow Wilson* (Baltimore: The Johns Hopkins Press, 1943), p. 101.

the full attention they deserve, probably because they were overshadowed by Jevons's work on marginal utility. No one who was not acquainted with Bagehot's writings could have been considered a serious student of central banking theory. Bagehot's work provided the rationale which allowed the Bank of England to operate as a central bank.

Wilson was also familiar with contemporary writers on money and banking.[3] Two of his colleagues at Princeton were interested in the subject: Royal Meeker and E. W. Kemmerer. There is little doubt that by 1912 Wilson had some very definite ideas about the banking situation and possible solutions. Glass and Willis tended to depict Wilson as being influenced by their proposals, but this portrayal is probably misleading. Wilson had a familiarity with the subject, and there was really nothing new in the proposals made by Glass and Willis.

Nevertheless, at the beginning of 1912 one thing was certain: the Aldrich Bill was dead. Everyone suspected that the Democrats under Wilson's leadership would propose a substitute, but it was unknown when and how such a substitute would appear. The bankers were especially anxious, because they had approved of the Aldrich Bill and feared that the Democrats might substitute legislation unfavorable to the banking community. They tried at once to ascertain Wilson's thoughts on banking and currency. Two bankers, A. B. Hepburn and E. D. Hulbert of Chicago, were intimate friends of President Wilson, and Hepburn often visited Wilson in Washington. On one occasion Hepburn related his discussions there to Willis. Willis later told Glass that Hepburn "made a desperate effort to find out whether your committee had drafted any bill."[4]

3. Ibid.
4. H. Parker Willis to Carter Glass, Dec. 20, 1912, H. Parker Willis Collection, Columbia University. All correspondence between Willis and others cited in this work is in the Willis Collection at Columbia University unless otherwise noted.

The Glass Subcommittee

In 1912 the House Banking and Currency Committee formed two subcommittees. One subcommittee, chaired by Representative Arsène Pujo, was primarily an investigative committee which was to examine the operations of the so-called "Money Trust." The other subcommittee was entrusted to Representative Glass and was supposed to deal with reform proposals. One of the first actions Glass took was to acquire the services of Henry Parker Willis as the subcommittee expert. Willis was best known as a professor at Washington and Lee University and as a financial writer for the *Journal of Commerce*. It is not clear whether Willis's part in the National Citizens' League propaganda campaign was known to Glass, since neither he nor Willis ever mention it in their accounts. The subcommittee met to discuss the problems which needed attention, but no public hearings were held during 1912. Willis and Glass seem to have forged ahead on their own to prepare a banking reform bill.

On December 26, 1912, shortly after Wilson's election, Willis and Glass met with the president-elect at Princeton. In his book, Willis gives the impression that he had already prepared a bill to be presented to the president for discussion, and claims that a draft of the bill had been completed in October 1912.[5] However, the account given by Glass and letters between him and Willis indicate that what they presented to the president-elect were merely their ideas about a bill. Other evidence indicates that what Willis calls the "first draft of the Glass Bill" was not completed until early 1913 and not shown to the president until February of that year.[6]

The Willis correspondence does make it clear that much of the bill which emerged as the Federal Reserve Act was already

5. Willis, *The Federal Reserve System*, p. 134.
6. Ibid., p. 1531.

in his mind by late 1912, especially the divisional reserve bank idea, which was the central organizational feature when the plan was presented to Wilson. One important difference between the early plan and the Federal Reserve Act was that Willis and Glass intended for the divisional reserve banks to be supervised by the comptroller of the currency, but Wilson suggested a provision which created a Federal Reserve Board to oversee the system.[7]

Glass and Willis give credit to Wilson for this idea, yet it could not have been new to them. Before Willis and Glass met with the president, Professor Laughlin had proposed a similar board in a letter to Willis, and Glass was aware of the letter.[8] Laughlin had prepared a plan based on a divisional concept with a treasury board for central direction which he called "Plan D."[9] Willis and Glass had seen this plan before their meeting with the president-elect.[10] If the Laughlin plan was the same as the Aldrich Bill, but with a new type of organization, it would have been very similar to what finally emerged as the Federal Reserve Act; more similar to the Federal Reserve Act than Glass and Willis's original proposal to Wilson.

Laughlin's plan was the result of a conference between him and Glass, after which Laughlin was asked to formulate a bill along the lines of their discussion. Willis, upon the receipt of this plan, replied that "whatever bill may be reported will be

7. Carter Glass, An Adventure in Constructive Finance (New York: Doubleday, Page, 1927), p. 82.

8. Willis to Glass, Dec. 12, 1912, and Dec. 19, 1912.

9. The bill proposed by Laughlin, in various forms, can be found in J. Laurence Laughlin, The Federal Reserve Act: Its Origins and Problems (New York: Macmillan, 1933). A draft copy of the bill, called "Plan D," can also be found in the Laughlin Papers in the Library of Congress.

10. Laughlin to Willis, Nov. 21, 1912, Laughlin Papers, Library of Congress; and Willis to Glass, Dec. 16, 1912.

the result of his [Mr. Glass's] own work and analysis."[11] Despite the reply Laughlin received, Willis mentioned Laughlin's plan in several letters to Glass during December 1912 and January 1913. A reading of Willis's correspondence makes it clear that Laughlin's influence was great. For example, Willis's letter to Glass on January 3, 1913, gives one the impression that Laughlin and Wilson were stronger advocates of the central board than either he or Glass.

Willis and Glass were quick to make changes and adopt the ideas of others. While this characteristic itself is admirable, in Glass and Willis it sometimes found an unfortunate counterpart in their unwillingness to give credit to others. Laughlin sensed that his ideas were being adopted, but that he was being shouldered aside.[12] In May 1913, Willis refused to send Laughlin a copy of the Glass Bill, claiming that "it would be manifestly the violation of my relations to Mr. Glass for me to send the bill to anyone or to show it to anyone without permission."[13] Earlier, Willis had said to Laughlin that sending him the proposal, if approved by Glass, "might be a very good plan as we should thereby get the benefit of your criticism and suggestions."[14] As a matter of fact, Willis and Glass had determined months earlier to keep the bill as secret as possible.[15] They were dismayed when a digest of the bill prepared by Willis for President Wilson, apparently at the request of Colonel E. M. House, a close adviser to the president, was given to Warburg to criticize. Willis and Glass were incensed that the bill had fallen into the "wrong" hands.[16]

11. Willis, *The Federal Reserve System*, p. 534.
12. This is indicated by Laughlin's reply to a telegram from Willis, Laughlin to Willis, Dec. 7, 1912, Laughlin Papers, Library of Congress.
13. Willis to Laughlin, May 17, 1913.
14. Willis to Laughlin, May 13, 1913.
15. Willis to Glass, Jan. 21, 1913.
16. Willis, *The Federal Reserve System*, pp. 191–193, 431–434.

The most obvious omission by Willis and Glass is their refusal to credit Victor Morawetz with originating the idea of sectional reserve banks. At the time Morawetz's proposal became public, everyone had hailed it as an original contribution to the banking reform discussion. Morawetz's plan was widely known, but one searches in vain for a single reference to it by Willis or Glass.

After the Federal Reserve Act was passed, Glass wrote a letter to the *New York Evening Post* disputing an account which asserted the influence of Morawetz. This action prompted a long letter to Glass from Morawetz, in which he denied that he had actually claimed any direct influence on the Federal Reserve Act. He did point out that he was the first to propose regional reserve banks and noted that he had sent revised copies of his article to the House Banking and Currency Committee and to the Senate Banking Committee in the autumn of 1911. In December 1912 a copy of the article was given to president-elect Wilson. Morawetz further stated that he had letters from two people, one of whom was J. Laurence Laughlin, saying that Wilson told them he "approved of the general plan which I outlined."[17] There can be no excuse for the lack of credit given to Morawetz as the original proponent of regional reserve banks. Morawetz himself, like most others with a legitimate claim to authorship of parts of the Federal Reserve Act, claimed nothing publicly until Glass's open attack.[18]

By Wilson's inauguration in 1913, it is clear that Willis and Glass had combined features from many bills into a new proposal. They borrowed principally from the Aldrich Bill, Mora-

17. Reprinted in Warburg, *The Federal Reserve System*, I, 588.
18. The attack by Glass was apparently caused by a personal letter written by Morawetz to Colonel House which was made public. It indicated that Wilson had stated to one of Morawetz's friends that Morawetz should be satisfied with the plan since it was his own. See Warburg, *The Federal Reserve System*, I, 590.

wetz's proposal, and Laughlin's Plan D.[19] Glass and Willis intended to refine and eventually introduce the new proposal into Congress. The vehicle for this process was the Glass Subcommittee and its public hearings.

The rest of the subcommittee's members, like Glass, had little banking experience. Two members, Robert J. Bulkley and George D. McCreary, later turned to banking, but only two of the congressmen who took part in the hearings had had previous experience with financial institutions. James McKinney had served as president of the Illinois State Bankers' Association from 1908 to 1909 while he was also a representative. The other member familiar with finance was J. Fred C. Talbott, who was insurance commissioner of the state of Maryland from 1889 until 1893, just before he was elected to Congress. Among the rest of the committee, Charles A. Korbley was a newspaperman, and George W. Taylor was a practicing lawyer. John J. Kindred of New York is a very interesting case; born in Virginia, and educated at the University of Virginia, he was a medical doctor who had studied in Edinburgh and founded clinics in New York City to treat mental illness.

Because of the committee's relative lack of banking knowledge, the influence of the committee expert, H. Parker Willis, was extensive. Like most committee experts during this time, his power was great.[20] The committee, led by Willis and Glass, held several meetings before the public hearings began. With

19. The latter was very dependent on the Aldrich Bill for many of its provisions. The materials used by Laughlin to prepare "Plan D" show that many provisions, particularly those relating to discounting were taken directly from the Aldrich Bill. In the draft contained in the Laughlin collection at the Library of Congress, provisions of the Aldrich Bill have been cut and pasted into an early typed draft of "Plan D."

20. This view is strongly supported by the Glass-Willis correspondence.

Willis as the instructor, these sessions were probably educational in nature. This education was needed, considering the
knowledgeability of some of those who were to testify. The
committee members needed some rudimentary grasp of banking and monetary theory to prevent the proceedings from becoming bogged down in useless elementary explanations; despite the lessons, this is exactly what eventually occurred. The
hearings demonstrated the difficulty of learning the fine points
of monetary and banking theory in a short time.

Letters were sent to many people requesting information and
asking if they would be willing to testify. The group invited to
testify was a varied lot, with bankers well represented. Warburg
and Hepburn represented New York bankers, and George M.
Reynolds represented Chicago bankers. Southern and western
bankers were represented by Sol Wexler of New Orleans and
by James Ferguson of Temple, Texas. Festus Wade represented St. Louis, whose bankers were widely respected. Small-
town bankers were represented by Andrew J. Frame of
Waukesha, Wisconsin, as well as Ferguson.

Public officials were represented by Charles N. Fowler, long
active in banking reform, and former chairman of the committee; S. M. Wilhite, comptroller of Louisville, Kentucky,
and Edmund D. Fisher, deputy comptroller of New York
City, also testified. The business representatives numbered,
among others, John V. Farwell of Chicago, president of the
National Citizens' League, and four delegates from the National Association of Credit Men, an organization of businessmen, merchants, and bankers founded to improve trade conditions.

Laughlin and Royal Meeker of Princeton, President Wilson's
former colleague, were the economists who were invited to
testify. The original list of economists, from which information
was solicited, included many well-known figures. F. W.

Taussig, Irving Fisher, E. R. A. Seligman, A. C. Miller (later a member of the Federal Reserve Board), E. W. Kemmerer, Horace White, Maurice L. Muhleman, William A. Scott, and others were included on a list sent to Glass by Willis.[21] Although Morawetz was not included on the list, he did eventually testify.

Agricultural interests were represented by the Grange and the Farmer's Educational and Cooperative Union. Glass and Willis discussed inviting John Mitchell of the American Federation of Labor, or Warren S. Stone, president of the Brotherhood of Locomotive Engineers, and drafted a letter to send them.[22] However, these men did not appear before the committee.

With a few exceptions, all those who testified were carefully screened. In some cases their testimony was discussed beforehand with Glass or Willis, to ensure that while witnesses were in some sense "representative," they would also be critics of the Aldrich Bill. This was not always possible, especially in the case of big city bankers. Almost all bankers from New York, Chicago, and other large cities supported the Aldrich Bill. In addition, some of the other people the committee was compelled to invite were strong advocates of the Aldrich Bill. Had the committee not invited Hepburn and Warburg—both well known—it would have been open to serious criticism. In one case, however, they were able to compromise. The committee had intended to invite James B. Forgan of Chicago, since Forgan could represent both the Chicago bankers and the American Bankers' Association, but shortly before the hearings, Willis learned from J. Laurence Laughlin that Forgan was going to refuse to consider any plan unless it had a central reserve. Laughlin also told Willis that George M. Reynolds was willing

21. Willis to Glass, Dec. 9, 1912.
22. Willis to Glass, Dec. 3, 1912.

to accept a divisional reserve plan if it was a necessary compromise.[23] Willis remarked, "I wish now we had summoned him [Reynolds] instead of Forgan but the plan suggested will I think rectify matters considerably. I believe that Reynolds will, *if he testifies as expected,* fully offset the influence of Forgan."[24]

When Willis and Glass were discussing who should be invited, they often showed their desire to load the hearings with anti-Aldrich Bill witnesses. Although he did not testify, E. D. Hulbert, President Wilson's personal friend, was recommended by Willis as a witness with good potential. Willis said that "Mr. Hulbert is a very sharp critic of the Aldrich plan and has taken an extremely destructive point of view with regard to it. I think he is one of the best men we could get."[25]

Among the country bankers it was easier to find critics of the Aldrich Bill. Andrew J. Frame and James Ferguson were selected in large part because they were known critics of the Aldrich Bill. In Frame's case, Willis wrote to Glass saying, "I think a good man to invite as a country banker and critic of the Aldrich Monetary Commission plan will be Mr. A. J. Frame, of Waukesha, Wisconsin. Mr. Frame is an intelligent country banker who has been prominent in the American Bankers' Association and has severely criticized the Aldrich proposition."[26]

The situation was much the same with the economists who were invited. Most economists, by Willis's own admission, favored the establishment of some variant of a central bank. Even O. M. W. Sprague, earlier a rather strong critic of central banking in the United States, in the end admitted that the idea had its merits. Sprague's name was not included on the list

23. Willis to Glass, Jan. 13, 1913.
24. Ibid., with emphasis added. Reynolds eventually did testify and Forgan did not.
25. Willis to Glass, Dec. 14, 1912.
26. Willis to Glass, Dec. 3, 1912.

sent to Glass by Willis, although he was perhaps the most knowledgeable of all contemporary economists regarding banking reform. His work for the National Monetary Commission, although written while he was still a critic of centralized banking, presented strong argument for a controlling body such as the National Reserve Association.[27] Eventually Laughlin and Royal Meeker, both sympathetic to a divisional reserve plan, were invited.

Evidence indicates that Glass and Willis attempted to influence the testimony of witnesses. In a letter to Glass on January 13, 1913, Willis indicated that he had discussed future testimony with at least two of the witnesses. Willis wrote, "I saw Mr. Flannigan today as you requested and went over his plans. He has some good ideas in mind and I shall be able to discuss them with you if you wish on Wednesday." Willis went on to say, "I have been over Fisher's testimony with him for Wednesday and got him to be as moderate as possible and I think you will be pleased with his testimony in the main."[28]

While there may have been nothing improper in the way in which Glass and Willis organized the hearings, they certainly cannot be regarded as an impartial forum. The subcommittee hearings were little more than the unveiling of the reform measure that the Democrats intended to offer to Congress.

The tone of the hearings was set by Glass in his opening statement:

This . . . is a subcommittee of the House Committee on Banking and Currency charged with the specific business of investigating, considering, and reporting some measure of reform in the banking and currency laws of the country, and we have invited you gentlemen here to give us your advice and opinions as to the best thing to be done. Perhaps I might say without impropriety that, speaking for the majority members of the committee, while we do not pro-

27. Sprague, *History of Crises.*
28. Willis to Glass, Jan. 13, 1913.

pose to restrict the gentlemen who appear in anything they may desire to say, it is nevertheless a fact that we must recognize and deal with that the party of the majority members has specifically declared against what is known as the Aldrich bill. However, if you, or any of the other gentlemen who shall appear hereafter, desire to discuss that measure the committee will gladly hear you. We would like to find out from you, though assuming that you think the Aldrich bill, so called, is the best thing to be had, what is the next best thing.[29]

Glass argued that since the Democratic party's platform had condemned the Aldrich Bill or a central bank, Democrats elected on that platform were obligated to uphold it.[30] Glass probably had no more attachment to this concept of representation than Edmund Burke had, but it was a very convenient method with which to shift discussion away from the Aldrich Bill, toward the ideas held by Glass, Willis, and probably President Wilson. Despite Glass's continual insistence that the committee had no specific plan in mind and that it did not necessarily have even a divisional plan in mind, he showed great skill as an interrogator. He always drew the testimony toward a discussion of the best way to construct a divisional reserve system.

Other questions also were discussed in the testimony, but organizational features received the most attention. Bankers' acceptances were considered at some length by various witnesses, especially Willis. His position is not clear, however. At one point, he admitted that the risk on acceptances of well-rated banks was nil.[31] Later he took the position that acceptances could constitute a dangerous expansion of credit.[32] In

29. U.S. Congress, House, *Hearings before the Subcommittee of the Committee on Banking and Currency*, Jan. 7, 1913, pt. 1 (Washington: GPO, 1913), p. 3. Hereafter *Hearings*.

30. *Hearings*, pt. 1: 73.

31. *Hearings*, Jan. 8, 1913, pt. 2: 106.

32. Willis, *The Federal Reserve System*, p. 163

the Glass Bill as well as the Federal Reserve Act, acceptances were limited to foreign trade.

Other discussion concerned the expansion of national bank powers, the entrance of state banks and trust companies into whatever system might be created, and better credit facilities for agricultural areas. These three matters were intimately related. The National Banking Act prohibited national banks from engaging in most investment activities. The prohibition was due, at least in part, to a desire to limit the national banks to commercial activities as much as possible. National banks located in rural or agricultural areas were not able to meet many demands for credit, especially not those which involved land as security for the loans. To circumvent this part of the law, national banks created "captive" trust companies. These trust companies were widespread and profitable. Sol Wexler related to the subcommittee how he and the other three officers of a national bank organized a state bank and trust company with $200,000 capital. The officers took the whole subscription. In two years, the original stockholders were able to pay dividends to themselves equal to their original investment. The trust company stock was then turned over to the national bank to be held for its stockholders.[33] Trust company ownership was not always handled in this way, but potential profits induced many national banks to organize captive trust companies.

The general consensus of the reformers was that an expansion of national bank powers was desirable. Since state banks and trust companies outnumbered national banks three to one, state bank membership in the new system was necessary. It seemed logical to expand the powers of national banks, and require any state banks which desired to join to meet capitalization and reserve requirements similar to those for national

33. *Hearings*, Feb. 5, 1913, pt. 11: 611.

banks. This standardization was expected to increase potential credit in previously hard-pressed areas.

Another topic—one which took up more than its share of time—was mutual guarantee of deposits by the banks. Some committee members pressed questions on this subject at every opportunity, and few witnesses escaped this gauntlet. Big city bankers opposed deposit guarantee on the double grounds that a good bank should not be responsible for a bad bank's debts, and that such a guarantee system would increase the likelihood of bad banking. The subject was controversial. Glass, along with many others, believed that it would be difficult to pass a reform bill containing a provision for deposit guarantees.[34] While there was rather wide agreement on the benefits of note issue guarantee, most people held that bank deposits were private contracts, whereas notes had a quasi-public function.[35] Resolution of this issue was deferred until the creation of the Federal Deposit Insurance Corporation in the 1930's. Most people felt that deposit guarantee was an issue separate from banking reform.

In the matter of organization, Glass and the committee obviously favored a reform measure based on divisional reserve banks. This idea was strongly criticized because Glass proposed a large number of reserve banks. The exact number was not specified, but it was on the order of fifteen or twenty. Paul Warburg pointed out the most serious problem: some of the reserve banks might not have enough capital to allow the reserve system to function properly. Some coordination would be required so the system could combine its resources in times of stress. Coordination would not have been so necessary if the reserve banks numbered only five or six. The reason for the

34. *Hearings*, Jan. 8, 1913, pt. 2: 147.
35. For this sort of argument, see Laughlin's testimony, ibid., pp. 138–149.

larger number of reserve banks appears to have been twofold; there was the desire, first, to decentralize control as much as possible and, second, to allow reserve banks to be more in touch with the banks and business conditions of their own districts.

The point was made that the banks should have as much information about local business conditions and the member banks as possible. Better credit decisions concerning any local paper or the needs of the banking community would be the result. Such familiarity would make decisions about discount rates easier and would allow better control of local money markets. This line of thought was simply an extension of the attachment to local unit banks. However, as Sir Edmund Walker pointed out during his discussion of the Canadian branch banks,[36] the same results could be obtained by having fewer reserve banks with more branches.

A primary reason for decentralization was the fear of large financial interests. However, with perhaps as many as twenty regional reserve banks, the stronger member banks would have been all the more influential. Any reserve bank centered on New York would certainly have been more likely to come under the influence of Wall Street than a larger reserve bank which dealt with a larger district. The degree of decentralization proposed by Glass and Willis might have made domination by financial interests more thorough than would have been possible under the Aldrich Bill. If a divisional reserve bank plan was to pass, a compromise was necessary between the centralization desired by bankers and the large number of reserve banks planned by Glass and Willis.

Most of those who favored a divisional system stressed that at certain times it might be necessary for banks to aid one another. In the likely absence of voluntary cooperation, some

36. *Hearings*, Feb. 17, 1913, pt. 12: 643–677.

sort of coordinating agency would be necessary. The most popular solution was a central board to oversee and examine the divisional reserve banks, and to coordinate the entire system. Willis and Glass, prior to the hearings, were at best lukewarm about the notion of a central board. The idea was pressed on them by Laughlin and President Wilson.[37]

Note issue was a separate problem. Although most bankers were willing to accept divisional reserve banks if their number was small enough, they were unwilling to give these banks the right of note issue. Instead they argued for a uniform note issue managed by the central board; again, the question was one of centralization versus decentralization. Proponents of the latter view argued that the notes were to be based on commercial paper and that the local reserve bank was in a better position to handle such note issue. The other side wanted notes to be as uniform as possible, so that the notes would be acceptable in all parts of the country.[38] If each divisional reserve bank issued notes and the paper of any divisional bank was suspect, its notes might not circulate. A similar situation had existed before the Civil War: banknotes often circulated at different values in different parts of the country. The discount generally varied directly with the distance from the noteholder to the bank and with the resulting lack of information about the bank's assets. In this area the hearings did have an impact, the Glass Bill's first draft established a central board of control, and the board was given note issue powers.

The First Draft of the Glass Bill

The precise date of the completion of the first draft of the Glass Bill is not easy to determine. Willis's claim that the first

37. See Willis to Glass, Jan. 3, 1913, and Willis, *The Federal Reserve System*, p. 147.
38. See Laughlin's testimony, *Hearings*, Jan. 8, 1913, pt. 2: 134.

draft was completed in October 1912[39] is doubtful. He maintains that after the interview at Princeton with President Wilson "work was immediately begun upon the presentation of a definitive draft of the Federal Reserve Act and the material which had been taken to Princeton and laid before the Executive was speedily woven together into a completed measure. This bill assumed form about January 15, 1913." Nevertheless, this bill is not the bill given in Willis's book in the first appendix, called the "First Complete Draft of the Glass Bill." According to Willis, the bill completed on January 15, 1913, contained a deposit guarantee system and no provision concerning par exchanges and collections.[40] The "First Complete Draft of the Glass Bill" has no provision for deposit guarantee but does provide for an exchange system of par collections. Probably this bill is the version redrafted after the committee hearings for submission to the president in February 1913.

The evolution of the Glass Bill would not be so interesting if it were not for some astounding claims made by Willis about the bill's origins. These claims picture the Federal Reserve Act as an original measure and not a descendant of any other bill, particularly not of the Aldrich Bill. Paul Warburg, in his work on the Federal Reserve System, spends a great amount of time comparing the two bills. Any comparison clearly demonstrates the degree to which the Federal Reserve Act drew from the Aldrich Bill for essential provisions. Parallels between the Glass Bill and the Aldrich Bill are even closer; with only a few exceptions, the Glass Bill, especially in its first draft, is identical to the Aldrich Bill. In the pages which follow, the derivative nature of the Glass Bill, vis-à-vis the Aldrich Bill will be seen.

The final version of the Glass Bill established a series of reserve banks, each with its own capital. The minimum number

39. Willis, *The Federal Reserve System*, pp. 134, 147, 1531.
40. Ibid., p. 147.

of such banks was fifteen. Each national bank was required to subscribe to the stock of the reserve bank in its district. Subscriptions were 20 percent of the paid-up and unimpaired capital of the national bank, one half paid in, and one half on call. Each reserve bank was to have a minimum capital of $5 million in order to begin business. The organizational provisions of the Glass Bill differed little from those of the Aldrich Bill. The Aldrich Bill had created a central organization with fifteen branches. National banks had not been required to join the National Reserve Association, but it is difficult to imagine them not having done so. The real difference between the organization of the two systems lies in the location of the capital—at the branches with the Glass Bill, and at the center under the Aldrich plan. The minimum capital of $5 million specified by the Glass Bill would have made it difficult, if not impossible, to organize fifteen reserve banks; as several witnesses argued during the hearings, some banks would have been too small.[41] By forcing each district to depend on its own capital, the whole system would have been weaker than the National Reserve Association in which each branch had at all times the capital of the entire system behind it.

One of the arguments for decentralization was the necessity of ensuring the representation of local interests. A second argument was the fear that big bankers would capture the operation of a centralized system.

A comparison of the organizational provisions of the Aldrich Bill and the Glass Bill reveals just how different they were. At

41. The capitalization requirements were changed under the Federal Reserve Act to 6 percent of the capital and surplus of national banks with one half paid in. Glass himself admitted that this would raise about the same capital as the original provision. See Glass, *An Adventure in Constructive Finance*, pp. 320–321. Also the minimum capital for a reserve bank was lowered to $4 million. See Chapter 10 for a discussion of the organization of the Federal Reserve System.

the local level, the directors of the divisional banks proposed by the Glass Bill and the boards of the branches under the National Reserve Association would have been similar. In both cases all but one of the directors of each divisional or branch bank were chosen by the member banks. The director not chosen by the banks was named by the central organization.

Both the Glass Bill and the Aldrich Bill created large national boards with smaller executive boards. The executive boards were to direct the day to day operations of their respective systems. Under both plans, thirty members of the large boards were selected by the divisional or branch banks. The Glass Bill allowed the president to appoint six more members: the secretary of the treasury, the secretary of agriculture, the comptroller of the currency, and three bankers. The Aldrich Bill had sixteen members in addition to the original thirty. Nine were appointed by the branches and seven by the president. Three of the latter were chosen from a list presented by the national board and the others were the secretaries of the treasury, agriculture, and commerce and labor, plus the comptroller of the currency.

The executive board of the Federal Reserve Commission was comprised of the six members appointed by the president, and three directors chosen from the Federal Reserve Commission. The executive committee of the National Reserve Association was made up of the three ex officio members chosen by the president from the list given him by the national board, the comptroller of the currency, and five directors from the national board.

Any claim that the National Reserve Association was less representative of local conditions, or more likely to be captured by banking interests than the system proposed by Glass and Willis, is difficult to substantiate. The composition and method of election were so similar under both plans that one can imagine little difference.

The Federal Reserve Commission was given specified powers over the reserve banks. Among them were the right to examine the reserve banks once each month, to apportion government deposits among reserve banks, to suspend for thirty days any reserve requirements, and to establish a graduated tax on reserve deficiencies. The commission was also given the power to require or permit the reserve banks to discount one another's paper and to evaluate once each month the paper held by each reserve bank. These last two provisions were responses to the criticisms of divisional organization made during the hearings of the Glass subcommittee.

The National Reserve Association's board had similar powers of inspection. Since there would have been only a single institution with several branches, no provision was needed concerning the allocation of government deposits. The graduated tax on reserve deficiencies was specified in the Aldrich Bill and not left to the discretion of the board of directors. Since there would have been only one institution with centralized reserves, no provision for the rediscounting of paper between districts was necessary.

The two bills had very similar discounting provisions. Both systems were allowed to discount, with the endorsement of a member bank, notes and bills of exchange having less than one month to run (28 days in the Aldrich Bill and 30 days in the Glass Bill). Bills maturing in 28 to 120 days could be discounted by the National Reserve Association if they were guaranteed by the local association, and bills running from 28 to 120 days could be discounted under the Glass Bill if the ratio of the cash reserve to total liabilities exceeded 50 percent. This restriction is ironic since Willis and Glass claimed that their bill gave more power to local institutions than the Aldrich Bill,[42] but it was the Aldrich Bill which allowed local banks to make the final determination about the soundness of securities and their eligibility for discount.

There was a basic difference between the two bills regarding discount rates. The Aldrich Bill gave rate-setting powers to the board of the National Reserve Association with a rate uniform throughout the country. The Glass Bill granted rate-oversight powers to the Federal Reserve Commission, but the rate did not necessarily have to be the same throughout the entire nation.

The two measures would not have had the same effects on the pattern of reserve holdings. The Aldrich Bill would have caused little or no change; pyramiding would still have been possible, and banks would have been required to keep deposits with the National Reserve Association only to the extent needed for collections and exchanges. This point appears to have been a major drawback of the Aldrich Bill.

The Glass Bill changed the pattern of reserve holdings and lowered them absolutely. The changes proposed in the Glass Bill were not as far-reaching as those eventually adopted in the Federal Reserve Act, nor was the decrease in reserves as great. The Glass Bill allowed for a transition period of slightly over two years. Country banks were to hold a reserve equal to 15 percent of their deposits, just as before. Five percent was to be held in their own vaults, and at least 5 percent was to be held with the district reserve bank. The remainder could be kept in a bank located in a reserve or central reserve city. After a period of transition banks in reserve cities were required to have reserves equal to 20 percent of their demand deposits. At least 10 percent had to be in their own vaults and at least 5 percent in their district's reserve bank. The remainder could be held in

42. Willis, *The Federal Reserve System*, p. 145.

their vaults, in their reserve bank, or in a bank in a central reserve city (New York, Chicago, or St. Louis). Banks in central reserve cities also had a required reserve equal to 20 percent of their demand deposits. Ten percent was to be kept in their own vaults, 5 percent in their district reserve bank, and the rest either in their own vaults or in the reserve bank. This change in the arrangement of reserve holding would have taken the system a long way toward credit reform.

Another difference between the two bills which seemed important at the time was the open market provision; the Glass Bill allowed open market operations in both commercial paper and government securities, but the Aldrich Bill was silent concerning open market activities except for the purchase and sale of government securities. Because of the emphasis on real bills, this difference was stressed by Glass and Willis. Willis considered it one of the major differences between the two bills.[43] Two factors lessen the importance of the issue: first, the original conception of open market operations by the system was based not on their value as a policy tool but on the income which they would yield in slack periods when rediscounts were low; second, the structure of the securities market and certain traditions concerning the purchase and sale of commercial paper eventually shifted open market operations into government securities anyway.[44] These considerations aside, the real reason for the lack of more general open market provisions in the Aldrich Bill probably was the influence of the bankers. If the National Reserve Association had been allowed to engage in wide operations in the open market, there would have been potential competition with commercial banks.

If the texts of the bills are compared, one can find more dis-

43. Ibid., p. 43.
44. This topic is discussed more fully in later chapters. See below, Chapters 9 and 10.

similarities. One example is the differing status of notes as reserves under the two bills. However, on major questions the bills are very similar. Both bills agreed completely on the notion that the note issue should be based on commercial paper with a partial gold backing. It was believed that such a currency would respond to the needs of business, and the idea that it might not never arose during the hearings.

The two bills were also in substantial agreement on organizational questions, even though at first glance they might appear dissimilar. The only real difference in this regard was in the location of the capital. The Aldrich Bill did not represent a centralized money monopoly as some politicans contended; nor was the Glass Bill a grass-roots banking system with complete decentralization. The Aldrich Bill gave substantial power to the local associations and branches, and its electoral process made it likely that Wall Street would find it difficult, if not impossible, to achieve control. The Aldrich Bill did create, however, a relatively centralized institution, as did the Glass Bill. The problems inherent in a system of divisional reserve banks forced the creation of a central board with wide powers; thus, neither system was really decentralized. From a political standpoint, the question of centralized versus decentralized control had been resolved. However, in both bills control was still primarily in the hands of the banking and financial community, since neither bill proposed direct control by the government. Glass and Willis certainly did not favor federal government control.[45] In the end, the question of government control and the question of a central board were both resolved by the president. Wilson was enough of a politician to know that the Congress would not accept centralized or decentralized control by bankers.

45. Willis to Glass, April 16, 1913.

CHAPTER 6

The Federal Reserve Act in Congress

The Glass Bill (H. R. 7837) was introduced in the House of Representatives on June 26, 1913, and referred to the Banking and Currency Committee. It was reported back to the House on September 9, and passed on September 18. On the same day it was introduced in the Senate and referred to the Senate Banking Committee. The bill was reported back to the Senate on November 22, 1913, and passed on December 19. Since the two houses passed different versions of the bill, a conference was called. The conference committee's report was accepted in both houses on December 23, 1913, and President Wilson signed the bill the same day. This chapter discusses the debate, compromise, and change which took place within the legislative process.

Initial Objections to the Bill

The first objections to the bill were not substantive, but rather aimed at the Democratic party's handling of the bill. Many congressmen, primarily Republicans, complained on two counts: first, they maintained that the Democrats had prepared the bill in secret, excluding the minority members from its drafting; second, they complained that the use of caucus approval had essentially deprived them of their right to amend the proposal. An agreement had been struck in the House Democratic caucus which allowed only Banking and Currency Committee members to propose amendments to the bill.

As for the secrecy charge, Glass and Willis attempted to keep the bill's specifics secret as long as possible and were very upset when information was leaked. Willis stated in his book that he and Glass had always been willing to discuss the bill's general outlines with responsible and interested parties, but that they were unwilling to discuss the measure's specific provisions.[1] This situation is ironic because their proposal would probably have gained additional support had it been discussed more openly. By refusing to discuss details, Glass and Willis frightened many interested parties, especially in the banking community. Bankers tended to believe that the reason for secrecy was the unfavorable treatment given them in the bill. Since the provisions inserted to ensure the regional system's proper functioning made the Glass Bill strongly resemble the Aldrich Bill, a more open discussion would probably have won the bill more advocates.

The reason the Glass Bill was handled in so secretive a manner is difficult to understand. Willis's contention was that he and Glass wished to draft a complete measure which could then be subjected to amendments. Willis felt that a more open procedure would have subjected the bill to special pleaders on every provision.[2] In retrospect, the handling of the measure in the House, where debate and amendments were limited, makes his contention a dubious one. Only minor changes were allowed by the Democratic majority.

At any rate, minority members were excluded from the meetings held by the committee's Democratic members, although Glass did keep minority members advised of the proceedings and solicited their views. The Republicans in both

1. Willis, *The Federal Reserve System*, pp. 191, 193.
2. Ibid., p. 193.

houses objected most to the use of a caucus vote to bind the Democratic members to the caucus report. Since the Democrats had a majority in both houses, this practice assured the passage of the caucus report in a virtually unchanged form unless the chairman of the committees agreed to amendments.

The Democrats had not developed a new method of railroading legislation through Congress; they had been educated in this procedure by the Republicans, who had used it with great success in the past. Its use had been most conspicuous in the case of the Aldrich-Vreeland Act. Since it was known that Representative Fowler intended to report a measure calling for an asset currency in 1908, the banking question was taken from his committee and transfered to the Republican caucus. By this method, the party leaders were able to produce the Vreeland Bill. The Democrats, who had objected to this process when they were in the minority, were quick to use it when they gained power and the Republicans were just as quick to object to it when they became the minority.[3] Such caucus action ensured party unity on important issues as recalcitrant members of the party were whipped into line. However, through this process individual initiative was blunted, and the probability of changing a bill after its introduction was negligible. Most members recognized this fact, and as a result, only a few members attended the debate.

In the House, another objection was that no hearings had been held after the bill's introduction into Congress. Glass maintained that hearings had been held, namely the subcommittee hearings in January and February. He claimed that

3. For such recriminations and counter recriminations see the *Congressional Record*, 63d Cong., 1st sess., pt. 5: 4668–4669, 4679–4680, 4688, and especially 4850, and also 63d Cong., 2d sess., pt. 1: 160–163, 169.

hearings had lasted for two months.[4] While the hearings did occupy parts of two months, Glass was stretching the facts, since total testimony lasted less than sixty hours.[5] His statement is even more astounding, since during the hearings he continually insisted that the subcommittee had no specific bill in mind. The hearings were in fact held on an early draft of the Glass Bill, although Glass refused to admit it.

In the House, debate was limited to four days, with the time divided evenly between the bill's supporters and opponents. In the Senate, where debate is generally unlimited, attempts were made to limit the discussion of the bill by setting a date for a final vote.[6] In the end, the bill came to a vote in the Senate one day before the proposed cut-off date. The decision to vote in the Senate was by unanimous consent, so it would seem that either all senators had finished their remarks or despaired of having any effect on the bill. In spite of the unanimous decision, all attempts to hurry the legislation along were pictured by opponents as proof that Democrats were determined to force their bill through Congress. For the most part, however, these charges were made as a matter of form, and opponents pressed on to more substantial criticisms of the proposed legislation.

Organization and Control: The Debate

From the beginning it was clear that the provisions dealing with organizational structure and control would attract the most attention. The debate centered on four questions: the number of reserve banks, the composition of the Federal Reserve Board, the composition of the boards of the regional banks, and the ownership of regional reserve bank stock. These questions often were found to be interrelated.

4. Ibid., 1st sess., pt. 5: 4894.
5. See *Hearings*.
6. *Congressional Record*, 63d Cong., 2d sess., pt. 1: 35–37.

The organization and control provisions of H. R. 7837 were an attempt to unite two opposites. On the one hand, in response to the presumed public distrust of the monied interests and the fear that such interests might gain control of a centralized system, these provisions created a system with as many decentralized functions as possible. On the other hand, it was realized early that a certain minimum degree of national coordination was necessary. The only way to ensure such coordination was to lodge a considerable amount of authority in some central body. The Federal Reserve Board was created to exercise this control.

The debate on the bill demonstrated the wide variation in the views held by congressmen. Criticism had three basic themes: too much control, too little control, and control by the wrong people. In general, the House felt that there was too much control, and the Senate too little, although partisans of both positions were found in each chamber. Members of the Progressive party formed a hard core who wanted government control from top to bottom. Republicans generally favored granting more power to bankers, and many Democrats felt that bankers were granted too much power already. Since the Glass Bill occupied the broad middle ground, most criticisms were offered by minority groups.

House Debate

Early in the House debate it became clear that some members, both Democrat and Republican, believed that the Glass Bill had gone too far along the road to centralization. One Democratic member, Thomas Hardwick of Georgia, lamented the fact that he felt himself bound to support the Glass Bill, because in his opinion it created a money monopoly. In his words, the Democratic party was giving as a substitute for the alleged private monopoly of Wall Street a gigantic monopoly that binds together all of the banks in the country, issues to them unlimited paper money from the Treasury in Washington on their assets, creates 12 great central banks, and puts a government board in charge of the whole combination. In other words, fleeing from the evils of Wall Street and a private monopoly, we rush headlong and pell-mell into the arms of a great public monopoly—a system that we create today, but may not be able to destroy tomorrow; that we control now, but that may control us before the end is reached.[7]

Hardwick was espousing the traditional Jeffersonian individualistic creed to which the Democratic party had paid obeisance for over a century. Hardwick's argument is reminiscent of Andrew Jackson's opposition to the Second Bank of the United States. Hardwick's own preference was a return to the ideas embodied in the Fowler Bill—the Canadian system of asset banking. This system would have maintained the relatively decentralized, atomistic banking practice of the United States, and would have found much support twenty-five or perhaps even ten years earlier. Now, however, this proposal received little or no support; the tide had turned, even in the Democratic party, toward more centralization and regulation.

However, there was still disagreement about the desirable extent of centralization. For the most part, objections were more specific than those offered by Hardwick. The most common criticism of the Glass Bill was the range of powers given to the Federal Reserve Board. Many representatives felt that regionally central organization was sufficient and that the powers granted the Federal Reserve Board, especially those allowing the board to require interbank rediscounts, were too strong. It was often argued that such powers made the Federal

7. Ibid., 1st sess., pt. 5: 4803.

Reserve System much more centralized than the National Reserve Association. Congressmen Franklin W. Mondell (R., Wyoming) and Horace M. Towner (R., Iowa) both held that position. Mondell stated that

the powers herein enumerated are sufficiently broad and sweeping to make it very clear that the Federal Reserve Board under this bill is an organization of vastly wider power, authority and control over currency, over the banks within the national system, and over the credits and business of the country—foreign and domestic— than the reserve association contemplated by the Monetary Commission bill. Not only is its power, authority, and control vast, but it is of a character which in practical operation would tend to increase and centralize. On the contrary, the authority and control of the reserve association under the Monetary Commission plan would be constantly checked and minimized by the influence of the local association.

Towner was even more emphatic:

This bill creates a "central bank." This plan is much more centralized, autocratic, and tyrannical than the Aldrich plan. It is true that we are to have 12 regional banks; but these are but the agents of the grand central board, which absolutely controls them. The power is not with them; they are not in any material matter given the right of independent action; they must obey orders from Washington.[8]

While these two were Republicans who might be expected to object to Democratic legislation, similar sentiments were often expressed by Democrats.[9] Since many Democrats accepted the premise that the people desired local control of local funds, it must have been difficult for them to approve of the extensive powers granted to the Federal Reserve Board. Again the question of party politics entered; Glass may have

8. Ibid., pp. 4691; 4896.
9. See, for example, ibid., p. 4862, where Representative Callaway (D., Texas) objected to the vast powers residing in the reserve board.

honestly felt that complete decentralization was best, but it is difficult to accept the thought that he deluded himself into believing that his bill created a decentralized system. About the only things decentralized under the Glass Bill but not in the Aldrich plan were the system's capital and reserves. These were probably the last parts of a banking system which should have been decentralized.

These obvious weaknesses may have caused Glass and Willis to grant the power which caused the most controversy: the right of the central board to require regional reserve banks to rediscount the paper of other banks during times of emergency. Bulkley, a member of the Banking and Currency Committee, admitted that this provision was necessary for the system to function properly; he maintained that it would be necessary whether there were five or twelve banks.[10] In a report prepared for the House of Representatives, Willis himself maintained that

it is evident that this power is not different in nature from that which is exerted by the head office of a central bank possessing several branches. . . . Those, therefore, who favor the idea of a central bank with a central head office, favor it because it grants just this power to dispose of the resources of the one section for the benefit of another, and must in consequence find themselves logically driven to a recognition of the view that such authority to transfer funds and to mass them at points where weakness had been indicated is properly to be exerted in the interest of the public.[11]

Willis admitted that such a power would make the divisional system function like a central bank. The important difference was that a central bank would back the liabilities of one branch with the resources of the entire system. The capital would reside in the central body, and no such thing as a debtor

10. Ibid., p. 4783.
11. Willis, *The Federal Reserve System*, p. 322.

or a creditor bank could arise. The Glass Bill created a system which gave the appearance of decentralization but whose individual parts could be coerced into joint responsibility during times of trouble.

Besides this spectre of coercion, many congressmen also objected to the proposal because they felt it violated the basic principle of decentralized reform, that is, local control of local funds. A major argument for regional reserve banks was their familiarity with the needs and credit of their customers. If the regional banks were required to discount one another's paper, they would be investing in paper about which they had limited information. Since the Federal Reserve Board defined "eligible" paper, the assets held by reserve banks should have been relatively uniform. Problems still might have occurred, however. For example, because of superabundant harvests, agricultural prices could move downward, causing existing agricultural paper of a reserve bank to be over-valued. Another reserve bank might be unwilling to discount such paper at its full face value. The Federal Reserve Board was given the power to force reserve banks to write off doubtful or worthless assets, so this particular problem could have been avoided.

The degree of centralization and the Federal Reserve Board's wide-ranging powers were defended by Glass and other committee members as necessary compromises. The description of the bill was dichotomized. On one side it was pictured as the Democratic and democratic alternative to an unwanted central bank proposed by the Aldrich Bill. In answer to the contention that the Glass plan was as centralized as the Aldrich Bill, the Glass Bill's supporters argued that advocates of a central bank should be satisfied with a system which operated like a central bank even if it decentralized some functions. Glass, Willis, and other supporters argued that the bill had all the advantages of a central bank while it eliminated many—or perhaps all—

of the objectionable features of such a system. The real extent
of centralization under the proposal was thus tacitly admitted
by Glass and his allies in their arguments on the floor.

The Glass Bill was also criticized from another angle. Some
Republican congressmen were only too happy to accept the
Glass Bill's centralization and its resemblance to the Aldrich
Bill; however, they wanted more power to be given to repre-
sentatives of the member banks.

Evidence indicates that Willis, and probably Glass, wished
member bank control of the system at all levels. That concept
had been a feature of their original proposal, but Wilson did
not believe that either the people or Congress would accept
banking reform unless the new system was publicly controlled.
His wishes were obeyed, and the Federal Reserve Board was
made up entirely of presidential appointees. These men were
either ex officio members by virtue of being cabinet members,
or the comptroller of the currency, or regular members appointed by the president for specific terms.

Some members of Congress merely wished a minority representation of bank interests, since member banks were required
to subscribe to the stock of the system. In the words of Representative Simeon D. Fess, "the Aldrich Bill gave too much
power to the banks [and] the Glass Bill gives too much power
to the Government or too little power to the owners of the
property to be administered." Other members, Representative
James F. Burke of Pennsylvania in particular, wanted all control given to men who were experienced in monetary matters.
He claimed they had served their nation well throughout its
history, and to exclude them from the operation of the system
was an injustice as well as a foolhardy action.[12]

The division was between old-line Democrats and old-line

12. *Congressional Record*, 63d Cong., 1st sess., pt. 7, Appendix, pp.
283–284; pt. 5: 4852.

Republicans with the majority comfortably in the middle. Republican Representative Patrick H. Kelly of Pennsylvania summed up the division very well when he maintained that the

dividing line will be that which separates the national idea from the individualistic idea and the commercial idea.

The gentleman from Georgia [Mr. Hardwick] and the gentleman from Texas [Mr. Callaway] have given able expositions of the individualistic idea, which is fundamental with the Democratic Party. They object to the centralization of authority contained in this bill and uphold personal liberty while they would enforce free competition. They have expressed the historic attitude of the Democratic Party. . . .

The gentleman from Pennsylvania [Mr. Burke] and others have given able expression to the commercial idea, which is fundamental with the Republican Party. They object to this Federal reserve board solely because it centralizes authority with the government. They desire a central authority named and controlled by the banks, and with that provision would give full approval to the bill.

But neither of these ideas meet the demand of the aroused citizenship of America today. . . . Now, the American people are turning to the national idea, the principle that this is a Nation created by the people, whose powers shall be used for the common welfare of all the people.[13]

Whether or not the majority agreed with Kelly's characterization, they did seem to favor a compromise which would provide the advantages of both business management and government control.[14]

Although the real bills doctrine did not come under direct debate in the House, there was some debate concerning the type of bills which would be eligible for rediscount. In general this discussion involved the complaint that rural credits were not being treated equitably by the legislation. Part of this complaint involved a misunderstanding of the act's dis-

13. Ibid., p. 4884.
14. See also ibid., 2d sess., pt. 1: 174.

count provisions. The Glass Bill specified that only bills with a certain maturity were eligible for rediscount, but many critics mistakenly believed that it referred to the original maturity of eligible bills. It was their understanding that bills running 180 days would not be eligible since the law allowed only bills with a maturity of ninety days or less. Many rural banks handled a large amount of paper with a total maturity of 120 to 180 days, and it was believed that much of their paper would not be eligible for rediscount. Actually, all their paper which met the other criteria would be eligible thirty or ninety days after it was drawn. Even though the average total maturity of a bank's paper might be longer than ninety days, at all times a substantial proportion would be eligible for rediscount. This matter seems to have been very difficult for many representatives to understand, since the complaint continually recurred.[15]

There were also attempts to liberalize other eligibility criteria. These were again efforts by representatives of rural areas to ensure that bank paper in their own districts would be eligible for rediscount. In Willis's words, the amendments proposed "the issue of federal reserve notes (which were to be government obligations) upon a basis which might have amounted to little more than that furnished by stored agricultural products."[16] Given the seasonality of much agricultural paper, this consideration is perhaps more important than lengthening the maturity. This matter was related to the argument that there should be fewer banks so that a regional bank would not hold only one type of paper.

The congressmen who proposed these changes either did not believe in the real bills doctrine or did not know enough about banking to realize that the amendments they offered had theoretical aspects which they did not comprehend. The latter

15. See, for example, ibid., p. 4888.
16. Willis, *The Federal Reserve System*, p. 361.

explanation is most likely. The House debate was on an extremely low level and demonstrated that few members had any conception of the bill's underlying principles.

Senate Debate

The Senate debate was in sharp contrast to that in the House; it was much more informed and intelligent. Willis expressed some surprise about this.[17] He maintained that since the bill had originated in the House it should be expected that the House debate would be superior. Actually, the fact that serious, informed debate was lacking in the House and present in the Senate should not mystify anyone. The House was presented with a *fait accompli*, and few members outside the inner circle around Glass and Willis knew anything about the bill's specific features before its introduction. One could not expect banking novices to become knowledgeable on the topic in the short time which was allowed for debate. In many ways, Willis and Glass were responsible for the lack of intelligent debate in the House.

In contrast, the Senate was given ample time to study the bill and hold extensive hearings. The Senate hearings were longer than those of the Glass subcommittee, and represented a more varied discussion of the proposed reform. By the time of the Senate hearings, the bill's details were known, and more specific criticisms and suggestions could be made. The Senate committee's witnesses included a better representation of interests opposed to features of the Glass Bill, and Willis, for one, believed that the Senate hearings were nothing more than a forum for the Glass Bill's opponents.[18]

It is true that interests opposed to the House bill received a more sympathetic consideration in the Senate than they did in

17. Ibid., p. 472.
18. Ibid., chap. 19.

the House. The Senate hearings brought forward a wide variety of opinion and reflected the general state of discussion at the time.[19] Witnesses ranged from the currency committee of the American Bankers' Association, to H. Parker Willis. Many who testified before the House subcommittee also testified before the Senate committee.

Except for a few cases to be mentioned later, the main goal of critical witnesses was more centralization. The American Bankers' Association's representatives were the first witnesses and divided various topics among themselves in order to avoid redundancy. They stated immediately that they favored a central bank or, failing this, a maximum of five reserve banks. For the most part, the bankers were unconcerned with theoretical matters. Their primary interest was the creation of a system more favorable to the existing banks. Even though the testimony before the Senate committee was not hostile, it did reflect some dissatisfaction with the bill as it stood. For the most part, the hearings before the Senate committee anticipated the debate on the floor. Nevertheless, in spite of more extended hearings and the generally higher caliber of the Senate debate, Willis asserted that the Senate achieved little in changing the original bill.[20] This characterization of the Senate's effect will be discussed later.

It was obvious from the beginning that most senators favored more centralization than was in the original House bill. The senators also were more candid about the true nature of the bills under consideration. Senators James A. O'Gorman (D., N.Y.) and William E. Borah (R., Idaho) argued that all three of the bills under consideration (the Glass Bill and two

19. See U.S. Congress, Senate Banking and Currency Committee, *Hearings on H. R. 7837 (S.2639), Senate Document 232* (Washington, D.C.: GPO, 1913).
20. Willis, *The Federal Reserve System*, p. 472.

proposed substitutes) in reality created central banks. Other senators openly advocated a central bank in name as well as in substance.[21] However, this step was blocked by Glass, the president, and a slim majority in the Senate. Most senators desired a decrease in the number of reserve banks and this was accepted as a compromise by the whole body. A close reading of the Senate debate suggests that most of the senators, particularly those who supported the substitute proposed by Senator Robert L. Owen, chairman of the Senate Banking Committee, recognized the Glass Bill for what it was. They realized that a few changes, such as having fewer regional banks, would make it as centralized as many systems proposed under the name "central bank."

The Senate divided into two groups; the groups reflected the division of the Senate Banking Committee. One group, led by Senator Owen, favored the House bill with some changes in wording and a few substantive changes, especially a decrease in the number of reserve banks. This group desired to retain the rest of the organization and control provisions passed by the House. The other group, led by Senator Gilbert M. Hitchcock (D., Neb.), favored government control at all levels, even in the reserve banks. The Hitchcock faction was more sympathetic to demands for an increase in the maturity of eligible bills. The Owen substitute, which represented the party line, eventually triumphed over the Hitchcock proposal, but votes were closer than in the House.[22]

In the Senate as in the House, debate centered upon the

21. *Congressional Record,* 63d Cong., 2d sess., pt. 1: 664–665; 528; 664.

22. For an idea of the differences in the three proposals, the House bill, the Owen substitute, and the Hitchcock substitute, see U.S. Congress, Senate, *Senate Document 242,* 63d Cong. (Washington, D.C.: GPO, 1913). In this document the three bills are printed in parallel columns.

bill's organization and control provisions. The consensus was that the House had erred in selecting twelve as the minimum number of regional reserve banks. The Owen substitute provided for not less than eight nor more than twelve reserve banks, and the Hitchcock substitute provided for four banks. It became obvious that the bill passed by the Senate would allow a maximum of twelve reserve banks.

Senator Joseph L. Bristow (R., Kan.) pointed out that the fewer the reserve banks, the larger the territory each would cover, and the larger the territory, the more diversified their investments would be.[23] With many small reserve banks, each one might depend heavily on one industry—cotton, corn, textiles, and so forth. Small capital would increase the probability that the banks would be forced to seek outside aid during times of stress.

Unlike the Hitchcock substitute, the Owen substitute changed the number of reserve banks but left the rest of the organization and control provisions substantially intact.[24] The Hitchcock faction objected to almost all the Glass Bill's provisions for organization and control. They believed that for the present, regional reserve banks should be no more than four in number. They were willing to allow for the organiza-

23. *Congressional Record*, 63d Cong., 2d sess., pt. 8: 528. This was exactly the argument given by Frank A. Vanderlip during the Senate hearings (*Senate Hearings*, pt. 3: 1933). Paul Warburg had already made similar criticisms of a digest of the Glass Bill given to him by Colonel House.

24. The Owen substitute did remove the secretary of agriculture and the comptroller of the currency from both the organization committee and the Federal Reserve Board, replacing them with presidential appointees. The Owen substitute also changed the capital of the system to 6 percent of the member banks' capital and surplus rather than 20 percent of capital alone. This change yielded almost the same total as the House provision but satisfied small banks which claimed the House provision discriminated against them.

tion of four more banks sometime in the future, if it should become necessary. They agreed that the capitalization of the system should be based on the capital and surplus of the member banks.

The Hitchock group's most radical departure from the Glass Bill was their desire that the stock of the system be sold to the public. Their plan allowed member banks to subscribe to the stock only if the public refused to take the entire amount. Directors of the regional banks would not have been chosen on the basis of stockholding.

The organization and control provisions of the Hitchcock substitute were interrelated: they stood or fell together. Since a small number of regional banks could not be tolerated if they were controlled by member banks, the substitute provided that the majority of the regional reserve bank directors would be chosen by the Federal Reserve Board. This provision would give the government top to bottom control of a more centralized system. The Hitchcock faction did not believe that member banks should be allowed to control the more centralized system which they proposed. In his opening statement Owen had maintained that banks were entitled to name a majority of the directors of the regional banks because they contributed the capital. Hitchcock's group felt that public ownership removed any objection to government control. In the end, Owen's substitute prevailed, mainly because of President Wilson's adamant support of the basic ideas behind the organizational features of the Glass Bill.

The Hitchock group also favored changing the discount provisions to allow longer-term agricultural paper to be eligible. Just as in the House, the proponents of these changes argued that most paper in agricultural areas ran for 120 days or more. The Hitchcock substitute provided that 50 percent of the paper discounted by reserve banks could have a maturity of between

90 and 180 days. The debate on this issue in the Senate was virtually identical to debate on the same issue in the House.

The rediscount provisions of the Glass Bill and the proposed substitutes were all open to abuse, since paper could be rediscounted as soon as it was drawn. The substitutes were more open to abuse from a banking standpoint, since they made longer-term paper eligible. Such paper would be much more illiquid and subject to greater fluctuations in price when the rate of interest changed. In contrast, the Aldrich Bill required any paper presented for rediscount to have been in existence for at least thirty days. This requirement was an attempt to ensure that paper presented for rediscount represented some sort of transaction and was not merely accommodation paper (noncommercial paper which was really a loan). The discussion in neither house covered the relationship between the rediscount provisions and the real bills theory, the liquidity of the reserve system, or any one of a host of other similar and related questions. All attempts to extend eligibility requirements seem simply to have been aimed at making credit easier for farmers. In the end, agricultural paper with a maturity up to six months was made eligible for discount.

There were distinct differences between the House and Senate debates. In the main, these differences concerned the degree of centralization the bill should specify. In the House, some members desired less centralization and in the Senate some members argued for more centralization. An interesting feature of the debate was the different way in which the two bodies viewed the Glass Bill. House members believed—or claimed they believed—that the measure provided a large degree of decentralization, but many senators saw the measure as a central bank in everything but name. This paradox no doubt explains the fact that the bills passed by the House and Senate were very similar though the debate was very different.

The House passed a bill which they claimed created a decentralized banking system. The Senate passed a very similar bill believing that for all practical purposes it provided a central bank. This duality was reflected in the Federal Reserve Act; it was possible to interpret the structure in different ways. This characteristic of the bill had an effect on the system's operation and development.

Conference and Compromise

Willis and others have maintained that the Senate had little or no effect on the Federal Reserve Act. Several points need to be considered to evaluate this assertion. The legislation presented to the Senate in the form of H.R. 7837 was based on a long discussion of banking reform and it is not surprising that the bill's general outline remained intact, since the proposal already represented a consensus of opinion on many issues. Had the act first been introduced in the Senate, the House would have had little or no effect on the general outlines of the bill.

The House and Senate disagreed on several matters and the Senate version of the bill was in conflict with the original Glass Bill regarding these points.[25] The areas of controversy included the number of reserve banks, the composition of the Federal Reserve Board, and the type and maturity of eligible bills.

Sentiment in the Senate distinctly favored a decrease in the number of regional reserve banks from the open-ended limit

25. By far the largest part of the amendments proposed by the Senate dealt with the wording and construction of the House bill. In its final form, after differences were worked out in wording and construction, the Federal Reserve Act resembled the Senate version much more than the House version, which was vaguely and poorly written in contrast to the Senate bill. For a comparison of the three different versions (the House bill, the Senate bill, and the Conference Agreement), see U.S. Congress, House, *House Report 163*, 63d Cong. (Washington, D.C.: GPO, 1913), pp. 34–90.

of twelve or more set by the House. The measure probably could not have passed the House with a limit on the number of reserve banks. Some representatives held a narrow, chauvinist view and desired the establishment of a reserve bank in their own districts. No one ever expressly stated such a goal, but it was denied so often that one suspects that it was in the minds of many House members. Glass himself probably did not want a great number of banks and was depending on the organization committee to keep their number down. Instead, the Senate limited the number of reserve banks to between eight and twelve. Glass's report on the conference suggests that the House conferees yielded readily to the Senate's amendment.[26]

The Senate bill removed the secretary of agriculture and the comptroller of the currency from the board. In conference, the House conferees were willing to allow the secretary of agriculture to be removed, but insisted that the comptroller of the currency be reinstated. This move was strongly resisted by the Senate conferees, but they finally yielded.[27] The independence of the system was a serious matter and the board would be less open to political pressure the more independent its members were of the executive branch, but congressmen realized that the attempt to make the system independent of the banking community should not be carried so far as to make the system simply the monetary arm of the executive. Therefore, probably largely for this reason, the Senate had removed the secretary of agriculture and the comptroller of the currency from the board. The tenure proposed by the House (eight years) would have allowed every president to appoint enough members each term to control a majority of the board:

26. Glass's speech is in the *Congressional Record*, 63d Cong., 2d sess., Appendix, and also is reprinted in Glass, *An Adventure in Constructive Finance*, Appendix A, pp. 317–336.

27. See Glass, *An Adventure in Constructive Finance*, pp. 318–319.

three cabinet members, plus at least one regular appointee. Such a composition might open the board to charges of political control. Under the Senate bill, with six members serving staggered six-year terms, plus the secretary of the treasury, a president would be late in his first term before the members appointed by him would be in a majority. Of course, by the end of his second term, all members would have been appointed by him.

The conference agreement returned the comptroller of the currency to the Federal Reserve Board. The five appointed members were given terms of ten years. The initial appointees were to have staggered terms with one member's term expiring every two years, thus no president would be able to appoint all the members of the board during a normal two-term presidency.

The Senate made two important changes in the rediscount functions of the Federal Reserve System. First, the length of maturity of agricultural paper was extended to 180 days. The House had originally limited all eligible paper to a maturity of ninety days, but then reversed itself on this matter and instructed the conferees to agree to the Senate amendment. Glass himself "agreed" with this change saying that the conferees yielded readily based on ". . . the conviction that sound banking instinct and universal banking experience will take care of the situation presented by this change in the House bill. In short, we are perfectly confident that those to whom shall be confided the power and responsibility of administering this new banking and currency system will have the wisdom and courage to maintain it in the most efficient state possible."[28] This statement is not so much an agreement with the philosophy behind the provision, as it is a belief that the bill gave the administrators of the system sufficient power and

28. Ibid., pp. 323–324.

discretion to cope with such a violation of commercial banking principles.

The Senate also changed the rediscount provisions to allow member banks to accept bills based on domestic trade. The House bill allowed member banks to accept bills only when they were based on the importation or exportation of goods. These bills were to have a maturity of six months or less. The Senate bill extended such acceptances to domestic trade but allowed Federal Reserve Banks to discount such acceptances only if they had three months or less to run. Both bills placed restrictions on the number of acceptances allowed each bank and the amount each bank was allowed to discount with a Federal Reserve Bank. The Senate bill allowed each bank to accept an amount equal to one half its paid-up *capital and surplus*. The same limit was placed on the amount any member bank could discount with its Federal Reserve Bank. The House bill allowed banks to accept an amount equal to one half their paid-up and *unimpaired capital* and discount an amount equal to one half their capital stock.

The conference agreed to all these changes except those allowing domestic acceptances. Senator Owen said that the argument against domestic acceptances used by the House conferees was "that small banks were apt to abuse the right of selling their credit in the way of acceptances by accepting domestic bills in default of any accommodation they could extend at the time because of their then resources. It was said that in that way they might abuse their credit, and that it would be difficult to keep a record of the sale of acceptances."[29] Glass and the other House conferees opposed even limited domestic acceptances because they feared that abuses might lead to credit inflation. After the change demanded by the House conferees, the *total* amount of acceptances allowed

29. *Congressional Record*, 63d Cong., pt. 2: 1470.

was the same. The difference was that domestic finance was discriminated against in favor of foreign finance. This provision also discriminated against smaller banks, since few of them engaged in foreign trade.

The rest of the changes proposed by the Senate were intended to give the system more flexibility and increase the scope of its possible activities. Three proposals in particular stand out since they, as well as a measure allowing domestic acceptances, were shortly to be added to the act as amendments. First, under certain conditions, the Senate bill allowed Federal Reserve Banks to discount the direct obligations of a member bank. Second, the House conferees insisted that member banks be required to keep a portion of their reserves in their own vaults, though the Senate bill would have allowed banks to keep all their reserves in their respective Federal Reserve Banks.[30] Third, the Senate bill would have allowed banks, with the consent of the Federal Reserve Board, to count federal reserve notes held in their vaults as legal reserves.

Within three years of the passage of the Federal Reserve Act amendments were added allowing domestic acceptances, allowing—and later requiring—banks to hold all of their reserves in their reserve banks, and allowing the discount of member bank promissory notes. An amendment permitting federal reserve notes to be counted as reserves did not come until later, because of the requirement that all reserves be held in reserve banks.[31]

30. This was not true of central reserve city banks which were required to keep one third of their required reserves in their own vaults.
31. It does not seem necessary at this point to give a detailed description of all the provisions of the Federal Reserve Act as it was signed into law in December 1913. For more information on differences in various bills, the reader can consult Willis, *The Federal Reserve System*, pp. 1531–1753; Warburg, *The Federal Reserve System*, pp. 178–424; U.S. Congress, *Senate Document 242*, 63d Cong., 1913; and U.S. Congress, *House Report 163*, 63d Cong., 1913.

CHAPTER 7

The Theoretical Background of the Federal Reserve Act

The real bills doctrine was at the heart of the banking reform discussion. So far, for convenience all the proposals have been lumped together on this account because, in all cases, they argued for commercial asset as backing for notes or credit. This chapter traces the development of the real bills doctrine and offers a stronger and more precise definition of the doctrine in order to classify various authors and their proposals. The real bills theory will be taken to mean that credit should be based on commercial bills and that such a limitation will ensure the proper amount of circulating media of exchange. One purpose of this chapter is to set out the background of thought which was incorporated into the act. Most studies of Federal Reserve policy begin after the act was passed. A few, such as those by Elmus Wicker and E. A. Goldenweiser, pay some attention to the background of Federal Reserve thought, but give it a somewhat superficial treatment.[1] A second task will be to discuss the real bills doctrine as theory, and place it in perspective with regard to American financial development.

In the United States from 1873 to 1913 there was a dis-

1. Elmus Wicker, *Federal Reserve Monetary Policy, 1917–1933* (New York: Random House, 1966); E. A. Goldenweiser, *American Monetary Policy* (New York: McGraw-Hill, 1951).

cernible evolution in banking thought, including a change in the definition of the types of assets deemed acceptable as backing for note issues. Earlier plans allowed notes to be based on bank assets in general, while the Aldrich Bill and the Federal Reserve Act allowed only short-term commercial bills. In addition, the real bills doctrine was extended to cover total banking credit instead of note issues alone.

The real bills theory first evolved out of a discussion of the issue of bank notes.[2] Even in the United States the doctrine made its first appearance in that context, though during the nineteenth century the domestic money supply was increasingly dominated by its deposit component. The United States, unlike other countries, had legislated reserve requirements, and as long as these requirements stipulated that reserves were to be held in "lawful money"—gold, gold certificates, silver, silver certificates, or Treasury notes—there was little connection between real bills and deposit creation. Once *deposits* were allowed to be counted as reserves, any discount of real bills by a bank with its reserve bank (whether a reserve bank under the National Banking Act or a Federal Reserve Bank) allowed a multiple expansion of deposits. With respect to the real bills doctrine, there was a difference between notes and deposits. This was recognized by Laughlin, at least. "Plan D" allowed notes to be issued based on the discount of commercial paper, but did not allow deposit reserves to be created through discounts.[3]

As time passed, the real bills doctrine came to be applied to the money supply in general and not to note issues alone. For example, the Federal Reserve Act allowed member banks

2. See Lloyd W. Mints, A History of Banking Theory (Chicago: University of Chicago Press, 1945), and Jacob Viner, Studies in the Theory of International Trade (London: Allen and Unwin, 1964).

3. See Chapter 4, pp. 84–85.

to satisfy a part of their initial deposit reserve requirements by discounting commercial paper and any subsequent reserve deficiency could be made up through the further discount of commercial paper.

While the discussion in this chapter will revolve around the real bills doctrine, the doctrine was only one of two distinct strains of thought which came out of the reform movement. The real bills doctrine has dominated subsequent debate concerning the reform movement and has been viewed as having had the greater impact on long-run Federal Reserve policy. The other strain of thought did not accept the idea that credit extended on the basis of commercial assets was self-regulating. This more flexible line of thought allowed much greater discretion on the part of policy makers. In fact, most Federal Reserve policy during the 1920's was based on this latter view, even though the real bills doctrine itself was never renounced completely. For a clear understanding of the evolution of Federal Reserve policy, it is necessary to recognize these two separate strains of thought and the struggle between their proponents for policy supremacy. They are two separate offspring of the reform debate of the period from 1863 to 1913.

The Real Bills Theory as Theory

The expanded definition of the real bills theory of banking is used here to describe a very particular theory, that is, that banks should invest primarily in short-term commercial bills (bills which represent actual production), and furthermore, that such a practice will allow the needs of trade to regulate the supply of credit without causing inflation or deflation. This theory should be differentiated from the notion, also common during the time, that a note issue based on the discount of commercial paper would allow elasticity in the substitution between deposits and currency. Henry Thornton's criticism of the "Anti-Bullionist" position should have been all that was required to point out the errors in the stronger version of the real bills theory. Thornton's argument was this: A sells $100 worth of goods to B at six months' credit, taking a bill due in six months. B sells the same goods to C, also taking a credit due in six months. This process can continue, and the number of bills outstanding will depend on the rapidity with which the goods are resold. If the goods are sold once each month, in six months $600 in bills will be outstanding, all eligible for discount, even though only $100 worth of goods have been produced. Thornton further stated that an extension of the customary length of credit, ceteris paribus, increased the number of such bills and concluded that this prescription for note issuing practice was a very poor one.[4]

Today, few would argue with Thornton, for it is realized that net additions to purchasing power, that is, additions not offset by leakages such as savings, affect prices and can give rise to further additions. This process comes about because at the new price level, expectations of further profits cause additional borrowing. If the natural or normal rate of interest (the profit rate) remains above the market rate (the discount rate), this process continues and a never-ending chase ensues.[5] Of

4. Henry Thornton, An Enquiry into the Nature and Effects of the Paper Credit of Great Britain (New York: Kelly, 1956; originally published in 1802), pp. 86–96; 252–253.

5. For a montage of writings which depicts this process, now commonly known as the Wicksellian cumulative process, see Thornton, Paper Credit, pp. 252–259; Knut Wicksell, "The Influence of the Rate of Interest on Prices," Economic Journal, 17 (June 1907), 213–220; and J. R. T. Hughes, "Wicksell on the Facts: Prices and Interest Rates, 1844–1914," in Value, Capital and Growth, Papers in Honour of Sir John Hicks (Edinburgh: Edinburgh University Press, 1968), pp. 215–256. The first two pieces are theoretical, Thornton's possibly the earliest statement of the idea and Wicksell's the modern statement. Hughes's article is an application of the theorem to the facts of economic history in England.

course, in the real world this probably would not continue in-
definitely, but the important point is that only through a sufficient rise in the market rate, which makes unprofitable some
prior production represented by real bills, can the inflation be
halted. As a result, credit limitations other than the qualitative
limit offered by the real bills theory must be developed and
used if a central bank is to eliminate large fluctuations in the
price level and other economic variables.

Acceptance of the Real Bills Theory

Despite Thornton's argument, English bankers continued
to profess belief in the real bills theory, whether they were
country bankers or members of the Court of the Bank of England.[6] The same was true regarding the majority of European
bankers, and, in general, American bankers and writers over
the last quarter-century before the Federal Reserve Act. As
time passed, writers in the banking reform movement in the
United States increasingly favored note issues based on bank
assets even though they did not necessarily believe in the self-
regulating power of commercial bills. When the National
Monetary Commission made its interview trip to Europe, it
found widespread support for such note issues.[7] The wide acceptance the real bills doctrine found among bankers and
writers, both in Europe and in America, persisted despite
many obvious ambiguities and inconsistencies which emerged
when the doctrine was transferred from theory into action.

6. There is some evidence that the latter group modified their views
over time. See T. E. Gregory's introduction to Thomas Tooke and
William Newmarch, A History of Prices (London: London School of
Economics Reprints of Scarce Works on Political Economy, 1962),
pp. 49–62.
7. United States National Monetary Commission, Interviews on the
Banking Systems of England, Scotland, France, Germany, Switzerland,
and Italy (Washington, D.C.: GPO, 1910).

The most glaring example was the inconsistency between the real bills theory and the gold standard.

The real bills theory maintained its popularity because, as Joseph Schumpeter put it, "it expresses very well the professional ideology of bankers."[8] Within the framework of the theory, bankers could maintain that they had no influence on credit or prices, because bankers merely served the needs of business and trade. Bankers obviously did not want themselves pictured as the men responsible for inflation and deflation; they preferred to appear as neutral intermediaries. Even Lloyd Mints, one of the theory's severest critics, allowed that the real bills doctrine had a "common sense appeal [which had] disarmed many writers and led them to approve the doctrine without critical examination of it."[9] His point was never demonstrated better than in the few decades before 1914 in the United States. The real bills theory appeared to many reformers to be an obvious panacea for American banking ills.

Mints eventually concluded that short-term debt and fractional reserve banking should be suppressed or eliminated, or, if this was not possible, banks should be restricted to long-term debts and equities.[10] However, Schumpeter probably represented a more reasonable position when he said that

finally it should be observed that there are elements of practical truth and wisdom in this doctrine. If reformulated to the effect that bankers had better be careful about their cash position and maturities and that they had better look with equal care at the soft spots in the applications for credit before them, it becomes quite unobjectionable. In other words, a faulty theory, in this as it does in other cases, covers wise advice. The proposition that sound

8. See Joseph Schumpeter, *History of Economic Analysis* (New York: Oxford University Press, 1954), pp. 729–731.

9. Lloyd W. Mints, *A History of Banking Theory* (Chicago: University of Chicago Press, 1945), p. 10.

10. Ibid., pp. 220–222.

business principles of discounting are all that is needed to keep the economic ship on an even keel should indeed have been recognized as erroneous ever since Thornton; but action in conformity with it would, nevertheless, have avoided all the worst breakdowns in financial history.[11]

The unobjectionable version of the theory, as reformulated by Schumpeter, was accepted by almost everyone who wrote on the subject (Greenbackers and such excluded, of course), but it is often difficult to determine who among the important figures in the reform movement went further and accepted the theory in its strongest form, namely, that short-term commercial investments would regulate themselves. The weak point in Mints's book is that he often fails to distinguish between the two groups. In many cases such a distinction is difficult, because often authors were ambiguous about their own beliefs, but the distinction is important because of its relevance to policy decisions and also its relation to necessary structural change.

The American "Banking School" and Its Transformation

The term "Banking School" is used here to represent a particular idea about the possibility of overissue of bank notes. "Anti-Bullionist" would work just as well. Both the Banking School and the Anti-Bullionists adhered to the real bills doctrine, but both groups were also concerned about matters other than note issues.[12] When American economic writers of the period from 1863–1914 are compared with either of these groups, it is only with regard to note issues. There were also some important differences between English writers and American writers. Though the American version of the real

11. Schumpeter, *History of Economic Analysis*, p. 730.
12. Mints and Viner trace the history of the Banking–Currency School and the Bullionist–Anti-Bullionist controversies.

bills doctrine clearly came down from Adam Smith by way of James Mill, Thomas Tooke, John Fullarton, and other English authors, it did undergo a subtle change. The basic theoretical apparatus was intact, but some American authors did not narrowly define the type of asset they considered to be eligible as backing for note issue.

After the National Banking System's first great crisis in 1873, the secretary of the treasury was able to maintain that there was a great difference of opinion concerning asset currency. Forty years later is was difficult to find a writer on banking reform who did not believe that commercial paper was the only proper basis for note issue. This state of affairs attests to the seductiveness of the real bills theory.

The two men most responsible for popularizing the Baltimore Plan the American Bankers' Association proposed in 1894, A. Barton Hepburn and Horace White, later were to class themselves with the English Banking School as believers in the self-regulating power of the real bills doctrine. Hepburn stated this directly when he compared two theories of bank note issue, the "currency principle" and the "banking principle": The "banking principle, which appears to me to be the correct principle, is that bank-notes should represent the credit of the bank, that they should be issued against the assets of the bank, and the volume thereof should be regulated by the credit needs of the bank's constituency."[13] White took the same stand in a 1902 address to the American Bankers' Association on asset currency. During a discussion of the merits of New England's Suffolk System, White remarked that it "is the public demand, not the inclination of the bankers, that determines how many notes shall be in circulation, and this pub-

13. A. B. Hepburn, "Government Currency vs. Bank Currency," in *The Currency Problem and the Present Financial Situation* (New York: Columbia University Press, 1908), p. 51.

lic demand ought always to be satisfied by banks paying out their own notes over their own counters in exchange for good bills receivable."[14]

The Baltimore Plan called for the repeal of the National Banking Act provision which required the deposit of government bonds to secure circulation. The plan provided for the creation of a new national circulation based on bank assets equal to three fourths of the paid-up, unimpaired capital of issuing banks. Included in the plan was a currency guarantee fund to redeem the notes of insolvent banks. The plan was a clear move away from bond-secured currency toward currency secured by commercial assets, but the scheme was still short of a complete real bills theory, since limitations were placed on the note issue.

The 1894 convention of the American Bankers' Association marked the beginning of serious agitation for banking reform on asset currency lines. While all those who supported such reform might not have been willing to go as far as Hepburn and White, the groundwork for nearly unanimous acceptance of the real bills theory in one form or another had been laid out.

The next important juncture was the Indianapolis Monetary Convention of 1897. This convention was not unrelated to the American Bankers' Association, although it was for the most part a representation of tradespeople. The convention's report, published in 1898, was primarily the work of one man—J. Laurence Laughlin of the University of Chicago, a firm supporter of the real bills doctrine. In the commission's final report, Laughlin stated that with a currency based on the assets of issuing banks the "volume of notes put forth under such

14. Horace White, "Assets Currency," *Proceedings of the American Bankers' Association Convention, 1902* (New York: The American Bankers' Association, 1902), p. 128.

circumstances will, like deposits, automatically expand in volume by being issued upon demand from legitimate borrowers, and automatically contract by being returned to the bank when the need for the currency is past."[15]

The bill proposed by the commission bore a strong resemblance to the Baltimore Plan, differing only in particulars. The Indianapolis Plan substituted an asset based currency for the existing national bank currency, provided for an emergency currency subject to tax, and established a guarantee fund. Both plans concentrated on note issue reform as the solution to existing monetary and banking problems.

Leaving aside the Aldrich Bill for the moment, the next major push given to banking reform came from the National Citizens' League. The theoretical arguments propounded by the league came principally from Professor Laughlin, the league's executive director, but also from H. Parker Willis and William A. Scott. Willis was Laughlin's student at the time and later served as expert for the House committee which drafted the Federal Reserve Act. Scott was later a professor of economics at the University of Wisconsin.

Laughlin's textbook on money, published in 1903, bears a close resemblance to the final report of the Indianapolis Monetary Commission, although the book is more theoretical and less historical than the report. The close resemblance between the two is not surprising, since both were written by Laughlin with the collaboration of Willis. By the time of the book's publication, Laughlin seems to have become even more ensnared by the real bills theory. He maintained that credit could be granted to the extent of the value of all property without affecting prices.[16] This view, which later may have been

15. *Report of the Monetary Commission of the Indianapolis Convention* (Indianapolis: Hollenbeck, 1900), p. 231.

16. J. Laurence Laughlin, *The Principles of Money* (New York:

tempered, took Laughlin far beyond the real bills theory; the doctrine appears innocuous in contrast to this position.

Scott was also a supporter of the real bills doctrine. In his short volume on money he says—speaking of bank currency—

Since it may be, and normally is, issued in exchange for credit instruments which record the current movements of commerce, it can, and normally does, increase in exact proportion to the need for it; and since notes return to the place of issue and credit balances are wiped out by the completion of the commercial processes which brought the credit instruments into existence, and at the time of the maturity of such instruments, it will and normally does, decrease in the exact proportion that the need for them decreases.[17]

Willis was one of the strongest supporters of the real bills doctrine. After working under the shadow of his teacher for two decades, Willis found himself in the forefront of the reform movement as the expert for the House Committee on Banking and Currency. In a description of the Federal Reserve Act written in 1915 to popularize the system, Willis maintained that "the law . . . accepts the banking theory of note issue rather than the so-called currency theory. 'No note issue without a transaction to call for it' is the first principle upon which the Federal reserve note is based. 'No commercial transaction that cannot obtain a note issue to facilitate it' is the second principle."[18] Willis was never to abandon his attachment to this theory. In 1936, in the last of the three major volumes he wrote on the Federal Reserve and central banking,

---

Scribner's, 1903), chap. 4, and also J. Laurence Laughlin, "The Theory of Prices," *Papers and Proceedings of the American Economic Association*, 6 (Feb. 1905), 66–83.

17. William A. Scott, *Money* (Chicago: McClurg, 1913), pp. 68–69.

18. Henry Parker Willis, *The Federal Reserve* (New York: Doubleday, Page, 1915), pp. 254–255.

he asked and answered this question: "What is the limit of expansibility of bank credit? . . . That limit is the ability and disposition of the community to absorb and use credit. The measure of that disposition is the amount of self liquidating paper presented to the banks for discounting or cashing."[19]

Both Laughlin and Willis at times took the real bills doctrine beyond note issues, extending it to bank credit as a whole. This approach emerged in the Federal Reserve Act and played a role in subsequent policy discussions. Both those in charge of the propaganda of National Citizens' League and the supporters of the Federal Reserve Act held to the strong version of the real bills doctrine, but, they also advocated structural change. For the most part these changes were aimed at the creation of an environment which would allow the real bills doctrine to function properly. Their position reflects two factors: the increasing theoretical sophistication of their arguments and the realization that the financial environment in the United States would interfere with the operation of the real bills doctrine. Despite the expansion of reform attempts into areas other than note issue, the real bills doctrine remained at the heart of the movement. Willis and others viewed the Federal Reserve Act as legislating the real bills doctrine as a policy guide.

To this point, the people who have been considered included the principal agents behind all the important late-nineteenth- and early twentieth-century reform attempts except the Aldrich Bill. Regarding note issues, this group would have been very much at home on the side of the Anti-Bullionists or the Banking School during the currency debates in England between 1800 and 1844. For their own part, these writers tended to associate themselves with the Banking School, although theoretically they were probably more akin to the

19. Henry Parker Willis, *The Theory and Practice of Central Banking* (New York and London: Harper, 1936), p. 26.

Anti-Bullionists. These American writers also demonstrate the intellectual evolution of the rather simple view that note issues should be based on commercial bank assets rather than on government securities, into the more sophisticated and extreme view that bank credit based on commercial bills would adjust automatically to the needs of trade.

The Credit Reform School

More consistent and also more correct than the above were the views of some of those involved in drafting the Aldrich Bill. These writers admitted the desirability of creating a discount mechanism to allow the substitution of notes for deposits, but they did not accept the argument that discounts of real bills would be self-regulating. Paul Warburg was the person principally responsible for the Aldrich Bill mainly because the bill was based on his earlier work. Warburg seldom discussed the theory behind his proposals, for the most part concentrating on practical matters and comparisons of the banking systems in the United States and Europe, but he was unable to maintain the discussion in a vacuum. At least twice he felt compelled to include caveats concerning the reliance any legislation should place on the self-regulating powers of real bills. In a monograph prepared for the National Monetary Commission in 1910, Warburg stated:

As the government banks from time to time buy this paper, the volume of their circulating notes, which they issue in payment, increases, while, on the other hand, when they collect this paper at its maturity and thus reduce their holding of discounts their outstanding circulation decreases. This means that they expand or contract according to the requirements of trade, because discounts represent progressive states in the process of commerce and industry. However, this is not merely an automatic process.[20]

20. Paul M. Warburg, "The Discount System in Europe," reprinted

He went on to describe the manner in which a central bank
regulates the volume of outstanding credit through the use of
the discount rate. Warburg had used a nearly identical passage
in a 1908 lecture.[21]

A. P. Andrew also rejected the hard version of the real bills
theory. Warburg reached his conclusions from his experience
as a practical banker, but Andrew, the economic theorist, had
reached his position from another direction. Several years before the National Monetary Commission was established,
Andrew participated in a session on monetary theory at the
American Economic Association meetings. The paper he gave
was a reaction to Laughlin's recently published book, *Principles
of Money*. Discussing Laughlin's ideas about the effects of
credit on prices, Andrew maintained that

the money values of things depend upon the amount of the means
of payment; and every enlargement of the latter's supply, other
conditions remaining unchanged, involves an increase in the former's value. Every new extension of credit, though based upon the
money value of goods, would tend to raise the price level, and each
elevation of the price level in its turn would justify a further extension of credit. . . . The alleged limitation of bank credit by
"the value of goods and property owned by borrowers" is from
every point delusive.[22]

Andrew's arguments, even though they came as early as 1905,
seem to have had little effect on the thought of Laughlin,
Scott, or Willis.

There is no longer much doubt that what was finally ap-

---

in Paul M. Warburg, *The Federal Reserve System* (New York: Macmillan, 1930), II, 193. Originally written for the United States National Monetary Commission, 1910. Emphasis added.

21. Paul M. Warburg, "American and European Banking Methods
and Bank Legislation Compared," ibid., p. 44.

22. "Credit and the Value of Money," *Publications of the American
Economic Association*, 3d ser., 6 (Feb. 1905), 111.

proved as the Federal Reserve Act owes more to the Aldrich Bill than to any other measure. Ironically, Andrew and Warburg on one side, and Willis, Glass, and probably Laughlin on the other, were able to agree closely on a piece of legislation though their theoretical views were far apart. The disagreement between the two groups was almost completely over the question of organization, and not over what each perceived to be the theoretical implication of the act.

Warburg and Andrew were not the only writers who saw problems in the regulation of credit through the discount of commercial paper. During 1913, O. M. W. Sprague, in anticipation of the Federal Reserve Act's passage, discussed the problems confronting the organization of the proposed system. The statements quoted below were made during a discussion concerning the need to ensure that the men chosen to superintend the system be competent in banking matters. In reacting to some unspecified claims about the automatic nature of the proposed system,[23] Sprague maintained:

Even in quarters where one might look for a clear insight into the fundamentals of credit and banking, a number of misconceptions are rife which if followed will inevitably involve the federal reserve banks in serious difficulties. That it is desirable that commercial paper be made a more liquid asset than collateral loans is generally admitted. But it has been contended on all sides during the last few years that credit could therefore be safely granted to an extent limited only by the amount of such commercial paper. Both of these contentions are hopelessly fallacious.

Sprague made his position on the hard version of the real bills theory even clearer when he said later:

The view that credit can be safely granted to the full extent of merchandise in process of distribution if not in process of manu-

23. O. M. W. Sprague, "The Organization of the Federal Reserve Banks," *Proceedings of the Academy of Political Science*, 4 (Oct. 1913), 106–117.

facture is equally fallacious. Credit affects prices. Liberal discounts may cause speculative advances in commodity prices, stimulating excessive purchases by wholesalers, jobbers and retailers as well as by speculative holders pure and simple. There is no mechanical or statistical test of the amount of credit which may be safely granted whether the loans are commercial or collateral. Overexpansion is possible in both instances.

Thus, Warburg, Andrew, and Sprague rejected the strong version of the real bills doctrine, while realizing, as Schumpeter noted, that it contained "elements of practical truth and wisdom." The discount of real bills played an important part in their proposals, but they were careful not to place too much, if any, dependence on the concept of self-regulation.

Assessment

The two groups discussed above do not represent all views on banking and monetary matters during this period, instead, they should be thought of as the poles around which most of the rest of the writers were distributed. We have concentrated primarily on principal figures in the reform movement, especially on those who made clear-cut statements.

The asset currency movement originated as a reaction to the inelasticity of a note issue based on government bonds, a characteristic of national bank notes. This alleged inelasticity was believed to have caused many of the financial problems in the nineteenth- and early twentieth-centuries. The proposed solution was a note issue which would better reflect the needs of trade, and thereby acquire elasticity. This rather general view of notes based on bank assets was transformed into the notion that the correct assets on which to base note issues were short-term bills of exchange or other assets which reflected actual production. Because these bills were payable at a certain and relatively near date, they were considered "liquid." Because they represented actual production, they were considered self-liquidating.

From this point, the two groups parted company. Warburg, Andrew, Sprague, and others realized that "liquidity" was not an intrinsic characteristic of short-term commercial bills. Unless there was some agency, such as a central bank, which could bestow this attribute upon them, they were no more liquid than any other loan: crises seldom coincide with the due dates in a bank's portfolio of commercial bills. An asset is liquid only if it has a market. Clearly a central bank should deal in credit which is due in the near future because its portfolio must be very flexible. So while there may be, as Schumpeter noted, characteristics of short-term commercial paper which make it the proper sort on which a banking system should rely, this is due as much to the institutional environment as to any feature of the paper itself. Warburg, Andrew, and Sprague denied that a note issue—much less credit—based on commercial bills was self-regulating. But they did believe that such a system could be operated to create a stable economic environment.

The other group—they might be called the real bills advocates—believed that the liquidity and self-regulating quality of short-term commercial bills were intrinsic characteristics. This group was, therefore, willing to compromise on the questions of centralization of control and location of reserves. The real bills advocates tended to give the impression that a banking system like the Federal Reserve which depended on the real bills doctrine would function almost automatically; this was the misconception mentioned by Professor Sprague. In their view, notes, or even in some cases credit, could not be issued in excess as long as they represented real commercial transactions. The needs of trade would properly regulate the medium of payment.

The main problem with Mints's *A History of Banking*

Theory is that he recognizes no difference between these two groups, because, given his assumptions about banking and credit creation, Mints had no need to separate them. As a practical matter, however, the differences between these two groups and their ideas have been extremely important in Federal Reserve policy-making. Since Laughlin, Willis, and Glass are usually considered to have had the greatest influence on the provisions of the Federal Reserve Act,[24] one might also assume that their adherence to the real bills doctrine meant it was transformed into law and then into policy. While the real bills doctrine is at the heart of the Federal Reserve Act, the effect of the doctrine on policy is less clear. That issue is the topic of Chapter 9.

24. See Gabriel Kolko, *The Triumph of Conservatism* (Glencoe: The Free Press, 1963).

CHAPTER 8

Economic Mythmaking and the Federal Reserve Act

One institutional change in the financial sector has already been discussed—the substitution of deposits for currency as the dominant portion of the circulating medium of exchange. Two other changes also were occurring. One involved the transformation of the American commercial credit market. This change was important because the Federal Reserve System was created to operate in a specific financial environment—one in which the real bills were created when commercial loans were made. The second change involved the role of the Federal Reserve and the American banking system in international finance. The international financial framework from 1900 to 1914 was based on the gold standard. Although the prewar gold standard was gone forever after 1914, contemporaries probably never had understood its operation. The casual acceptance the gold standard found in the minds of the framers of reform legislation certainly indicates such a lack of understanding. These two institutions, real bills and the international gold standard, were integral components of the structure of reform under the Federal Reserve Act, but by the time the act was passed, there was some question about their practical relevance to banking reform.

The Real Bills Doctrine

The real bills doctrine was the cornerstone of domestic reform under the Federal Reserve Act. The impact of this doctrine on the act's theoretical structure has been minimized by some writers, just as its effect on subsequent policy has been overstated. A study of the process which led to the passage of the act and, in particular, a study of the thought of those who drafted the act, can leave little doubt that the real bills doctrine was an important part of the framework of banking and financial reform.[1] At the time, there was a great desire to ensure that credit granted by the Federal Reserve would be for "productive" purposes only and would exclude loans for speculative purposes. The act contains an implicit statement that such a qualitative credit restriction would guarantee the correct amount of circulating media of exchange. This idea is, in a sense, a quantity theory of money, but is clearly different from what economists have called "the quantity theory of money." The theoretical inadequacies of the real bills doctrine are well known.[2] Even if the real bills theory was not an important part of the Federal Reserve Act, it cannot be denied that real bills were the mechanism by which domestic credit policy was to be implemented. It was the intention of banking reformers, whether or not they accepted the real bills doctrine, that commercial bills should become the principal medium by which policy was effected. Even this view of real bills posed problems, some of which were recognized by the reformers, but the magnitude of these operational difficulties was not recognized.

The term "commercial bill" meant a two-name bill of exchange drawn by one person or firm and accepted by another person, firm, or bank. In most cases, such a bill carried with it some evidence showing that it represented actual production

1. See Chapter 7.
2. Ibid.

of goods. Any application of the real bills theory to central banking depends upon the existence of such assets.

The Bank of England's operations on the London bill market provided the source for virtually all models of banking reform. Unfortunately few if any writers understood the mechanics of the English system. As a result, an idealized version came to be widely accepted. American writers usually did not realize the difficulty with which the Bank of England effected any major policy,[3] but simply seized on the success of the Bank of England and, using the idealized version of the bank's operations on the bill market, proposed a similar system for the United States. At least two problems were overlooked. First, instead of providing a medium for orderly monetary relations, the English bill of exchange actually caused substantial instability in the monetary system.[4] Second, the American financial sector was very different from the English.

Commercial practice in the United States ordinarily did not give rise to commercial bills of exchange, nor to banker's acceptances, since national banks were forbidden by law to accept drafts drawn by their customers. For the most part, however, prevailing credit practices rather than any legal prohibition caused the absence of such bills.

Two-name bills, both promissory notes and trade bills, had been used extensively before the Civil War. Credit practice in the United States was much like that of any other country, although it may not have been as well developed as in some European nations. With the beginning of the war the situation changed. The conflict caused monetary and economic uncertainties which, when combined with government monetary

3. For some idea of these difficulties, see R. S. Sayers, *Bank of England Operations, 1890–1914* (London: King, 1936).
4. See J. R. T. Hughes, *Fluctuations in Trade, Industry and Finance* (Oxford: Clarendon, 1960), pp. 256–274.

policy, made merchants unwilling to grant credit to purchasers. Partly for this reason, merchants began offering discounts for cash payments; if a buyer paid within a specified time, he received a discount on his purchase.[5] The result was a marked decline in the use of two-name bills. This decline is pictured in Charts 8.1 and 8.2. In fact, two-name bills were increasingly used to collect bad debts and became known as questionable investments. In this connection it is interesting to note that in New York City the peak years for two-name bills were also panic years—1884, 1893, and 1907 (see Chart 8.2).

The trend toward cash discounts was only one factor in the decline of two-name bills. The disappearance of standard commercial bills was also related to more general developments in the economy and society. Foremost among these changes were rapid developments in transportation and communication. Before the advent of modern communication and transportation systems, merchants tended to hold larger inventories and make only a few purchasing trips each year. Since stock was sold slowly, it was very inconvenient for a merchant to make a cash payment every time he received a shipment of goods. The result was the bill of exchange. As transportation and communication developed, improvements in market information decreased inventories, and the increased frequency of purchases made the bill of exchange less useful.[6] Also, as banking became

5. See Margaret Myers, *New York Money Market* (New York: Columbia University Press, 1931), chap. 15; Albert O. Greef, *The Commercial Paper House in the United States* (Cambridge: Harvard University Press, 1938), chap. 2; Chester A. Phillips, *Bank Credit* (New York: Macmillan, 1921), chap. 7; and J. L. Laughlin, "The Aldrich-Vreeland Act," *Journal of Political Economy*, 16 (Oct. 1908), 489–513. All of the above writers but Phillips agree that the cash discount system began with the Civil War. Phillips places it slightly later, around 1880.

6. The United States was not the only country which experienced a relative decline in two-name bills of exchange. This trend also occurred

more sophisticated and bank credit departments improved, the risks involved in granting unsecured loans declined. Banks were able to grant loans more often and at lower rates.

The standard interpretation of that phenomenon is that two-name bills were replaced by single-name bills, the latter representing loans made to take advantage of cash discounts. However, the trend of single-name bills shown in Charts 8.1 and 8.2 disputes this view. During the period of most rapid decine in two-name bills—before 1899—single-name bills do not show any large increase. The number of single-name bills did increase rapidly in that period, but the percentage did not. In fact, for all national banks, the beginning of a relative increase in single-name bills occurred at precisely the same time that the decrease in the proportion of two-name bills ended.[7]

In the United States, national bank portfolios reflected the change in commercial practice. While national banks made up only about one half of the total bank capital in the United States, in most commercial centers they were the heart of the

---

in the English credit system during the last three decades of the nineteenth century. See W. T. C. King, *History of the London Discount Market* (London: Routledge, 1936), p. 39, and Hughes, *Fluctuations in Trade, Industry and Finance*, p. 274. In his book *The Decline of Inland Bills of Exchange in the London Money Market* (Cambridge: University Press, 1971), Shizuya Nishimura traces the main reasons for the decline of such bills in England to improvements in communication and transportation. His arguments are very similar to those used to explain the American experience in Greef, *Commercial Paper Houses*, pp. 65–78. The English experience was not exactly the same as the American, however. In England domestic bills tended to disappear from the market in any form. They were replaced by foreign bills, which dominated the bill market during the last few decades before World War I. Instead of using single-name bills in domestic trade, it was the practice of English banks to lend by allowing overdrafts to their customers. See Nishimura, *The Decline of Inland Bills*, chap. 5.

7. Compare references in footnote 5.

Chart 8.1. Single- and double-name paper as a percentage of total loans and investments, all national banks, 1883–1914.

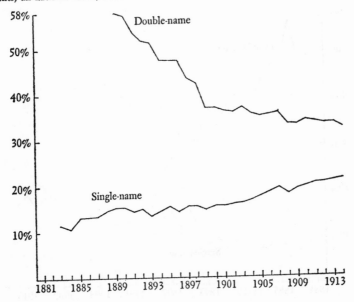

Charts 8.1–8.3 were constructed from information in the *Annual Report of the Comptroller of the Currency.* For all national banks, the *Reports* separate double-name bills from other loans after 1888 only. Double-name paper is segregated from other loans for New York City national banks before 1889, and some of these earlier years are given in Chart 8.2. Even though the description of loans classed as double- or single-name changed several times from 1889 to 1914, one can distinguish the two groups. After 1914 double- and single-name paper were listed in a single series, presumably reflecting the fact that both types of paper were equally eligible for discount at the Federal Reserve. These statistics are for national banks only and therefore represent but a portion of the American banking community. The consensus was that state banks were even less involved in the market for two-name bills. See, for example, Joseph J. Klein, "Commercial Importance of Single Name Paper," *Annalist,* 3 (March 23, 1914), 361.

banking community. The National Banking Act intended them to be commercial banks. Any decline in the percentage of their portfolios invested in what had historically been the basis of commercial banking is an indication of the change in American banking and credit practice. Chart 8.3 shows the

Chart 8.2. Single- and double-name paper as a percentage of total loans and investments, New York City national banks, 1881–1914.

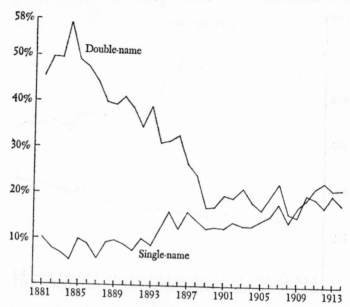

relative decline of commercial paper in national bank portfolios. Notice the parallel between the decline of commercial paper and the decrease in two-name bills.

There is one other interesting facet of the trend of commercial credit. Chart 8.3 also shows the movement of commercial credit as a percentage of total loans and investments for the first ten years of the Federal Reserve System. Though it is true that this period was not normal for several reasons, commercial paper shows a marked instability compared to the previous quarter century. Apparently, the Federal Reserve System caused no substantial increase in the stability of commercial credit. New York banks show a particularly high degree of instability. Throughout this period, the Federal Reserve Bank of New York was attempting to create a functioning acceptance market. The increase in the commercial portion of

Chart 8.3. Commercial paper as a percentage of total loans and investments, New York City national banks and all national banks, 1886–1923.

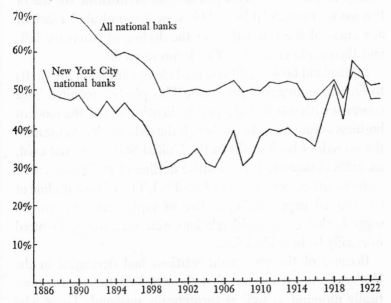

the portfolios of New York City national banks was accompanied by this increase in instability. The pattern is similar to that found by J. R. T. Hughes in English banks during the 1850's.[8] The questionable aspects of commercial paper were apparent earlier in the tendency of New York City banks to hold larger amounts of such paper during panics. During the panic of 1920, commercial paper comprised a larger percentage of total loans and investments of New York City national banks than at any time during the previous thirty-five years.

The decline in the importance of two-name bills was not perceived correctly by contemporary writers. The absence of two-name bills was considered to be characteristic of a poor credit system. Many believed that the creation of a central

8. Hughes, *Fluctuations in Trade, Industry and Finance*, pp. 256–274.

discount institution would almost automatically bring about a change in prevailing credit practices and reinstitute the use of two-name commercial bills. This view demonstrated a lack of awareness of the true nature of the decline of two-name bills and their replacement by other forms of credit.

In England book credit was used along with bank overdrafts to finance commercial purchases. This practice required large concerns with substantial liquidity, in other words, the modern business corporation. Even though the data needed to measure the growth of book credit in the United States may not exist, an indirect measure is the relative decline of traditional credit instruments demonstrated by Chart 8.3. The relative decline of commercial paper during a time of rapid economic growth suggests that commercial relations were increasingly financed internally by individual firms.

Because of the way credit relations had developed in the United States, it appears that the real bills theory was practically unsound as well as theoretically unsound. Those who proposed the real bills doctrine as a guide to policy, or even the discount of real bills as a method to achieve policy goals, were ignoring not only the doctrine's theoretical inadequacies, but also recent developments in credit relations. This latter problem was not caused simply by a change in the type of bill used as a credit instrument, but was also linked to the tendency for all traditional forms of credit to disappear. They were being replaced by new methods of credit extension which did not give rise to negotiable instruments.

The Gold Standard and the Bank of England

With regard to international finance, the Federal Reserve Act reaffirmed the Gold Standard Act of 1900 in a very casual manner.[9] The gold standard was just as casually accepted by virtually all economists and politicians during the pre-World

9. See section 26 of the bill.

War I period. If any one economic mechanism had been enshrined, it was the gold standard. But, just as in the case of the discount mechanism, accepted doctrine did not reflect reality.

Central bankers were presumed to follow the "rules of the game."[10] Since all countries on the gold standard held gold reserves against their currency (at least against all that amount above some statutory limit), when gold flowed out of a country, the banks in that country suffered a decline in reserves. As reserves shrank, credit was restricted through central bank changes in the rate of discount, and the note issue reduced as loans were paid off and not renewed. The gold outflow stopped because the rise in the central bank discount rate caused interest rates to rise and the decline in the money supply caused prices to fall. The fall in prices presumably caused the terms of trade to reverse and the upward movement of interest rates induced short-term capital to flow into the country. Most important was the belief that the central bank could solve the problem through discount rate policy. Furthermore, the "rules of the game" worked the opposite way for countries gaining gold. They were expected to reduce their discount rate.

In addition, bank action was presumed to be passive. The central bank was supposed to act only in the face of continued loss of reserves—which threatened convertibility—and not respond in a deliberate offsetting manner to changes in the international economic situation. The bank was supposed to swallow the pill no matter how bitter it might be. When the United States returned to central banking in 1914, this view was widely accepted. The discount rate was made a chief tool of the system, and the Gold Standard Act of 1900 was explicitly reaffirmed. The system was required to keep reserves in gold

10. See Arthur Bloomfield, *Monetary Policy Under the Gold Standard, 1880–1914* (New York: Federal Reserve Bank of New York, 1959), chap. 5. In this book Bloomfield discusses the extent of central bank adherence to the "rules of the game."

for its note issue and for the deposits it held for member banks.

There existed a widespread belief about the efficacy of changes in central bank discount rates and a faulty perception of the operation of the gold standard itself. The rest of this section discusses the operations of the premier central bank, the Bank of England, to show how bank rate and the gold standard interacted and operated from 1890 to 1914. The Bank of England's reactions to international stimuli were much more complex than a simple change in its discount rate. The bank was not averse to taking precautionary action in light of political situations or in consideration of the domestic economy, and often chose not to swallow the pill at all, or at least to sugar-coat it by taking actions outside the rules of the game.

Bank Rate

From a reading of most accounts of the gold standard one would suppose that bank rate was the only tool the Bank of England used to ensure convertibility. For instance, the Cunliffe Committee Report of 1918 is couched in these terms:

If the process [exchange of notes for gold] was repeated sufficiently often to reduce the ratio [reserves to deposits] in a degree considered dangerous, the Bank raised its rate of discount. The raising of the discount rate had the immediate effect of retaining money here which would have been remitted abroad and of attracting remittances from abroad to take advantage of the higher rate, thus checking the outflow of gold and even reversing the stream.[11]

Certainly, a tool which worked this well would be all a central bank would require. There are, however, other things to consider, namely the actual effectiveness of bank rate and its impact on domestic trade.

11. T. E. Gregory, ed., *Select Statutes, Documents and Reports Relating to British Banking, 1832–1928* (Oxford: University Press, 1929), II, 336.

But first, how did this view of bank rate come about? One source could have been the interview of the governor of the Bank of England with the National Monetary Commission of the United States in 1910.

Q. Do you regard prompt and adequate increase in the bank rate as the most effective measure to protect the bank's reserve?

A. Yes.[12]

What could be simpler? This was an unqualified answer by the governor to a straightforward question. Fifteen years before the governor would probably not have given such an unqualified answer to the same question; until almost the turn of the century, bank rate had been ineffective unless additional action was taken.

Any discussion of the actions the Bank of England took to make bank rate effective must include the constraints—traditional or otherwise—under which the bank operated.[13] First of all, unlike modern central banks, the Bank of England, according to testimony before the National Monetary Commission, never bought bills in the market place.

Q. Do you sometimes purchase "prime bills" in the market at a lower rate than bank rate?

A. The bank does not purchase bills in the market.[14]

In other words, the only bills "purchased" by the Bank of England were those brought to it for rediscount during the usual course of business by its customers in the London money market.

12. U.S. National Monetary Commission, *Interviews on the Banking and Currency Systems of England, Scotland, France, Germany, Switzerland, and Italy* (Washington, D.C.: GPO, 1910) p. 23.

13. For more detail see King, *History of the London Discount Market*; Sayers, *Bank of England Operations*.

14. U.S. National Monetary Commission, p. 23.

The Bank of England, once it purchased a bill, held that bill until maturity. The financial community knew that the bank would not purchase bills with more than a certain amount of time to run even though the exact currency allowed might be subject to change depending on the economic situation. Writers have often supposed that the bank bought and sold consols in order to make bank rate effective. However, a lack of evidence as well as testimony before the National Monetary Commission of the United States,[15] indicates that the Bank of England rarely indulged in this sort of action.

When the bank wanted to make the discount rate effective, it borrowed funds in the market, leaving security for the loan. This procedure obviously is the equivalent of modern open market operations, at least on the selling side. Such action allowed the bank to tighten the market without engaging in what it considered dubious practice. The bank generally entered the market through a broker, but later the Bank of England also borrowed from the clearing banks.

It is clear that the simple act of raising bank rate was not the only reaction of the bank when its reserve position changed. In fact, had changes in the discount rate been the bank's only reaction, the impact would have been quite different. Another very different tool was also used—operations on the gold market.

Operations on the Gold Market

The Bank of England's operations on the gold market have been neglected by almost all writers when considering the international gold standard. One great exception is R. S. Sayers, who in his book *Bank of England Operations, 1890–1914*, considers the matter in some detail. Sayers's evidence comes from various editions of the *Statist* and the *Economist*,

15. Ibid., p. 29.

as well as from testimony given before the National Monetary Commission.

Three methods were used by the Bank of England when it wished to effect the price of gold. First, the bank could advance its purchase price for gold above the statutory minimum of three pounds, seventeen shillings, nine pence per ounce. A second method of affecting gold prices was to grant interest-free advances to gold importers, although the bank required adequate security to be lodged. A third practice was the custom of sifting out light-weight sovereigns which were nonetheless still of legal weight and using those coins to satisfy people demanding gold in exchange for notes. This practice—not formally admitted by the bank—effectively raised the price of gold since it was not profitable to melt underweight sovereigns into bullion for export.

Whenever the Bank of England manipulated the price of gold, whether it advanced its buying price for gold or made gold importation cheaper, it was also manipulating the gold points. (The gold points determine the range over which the price of gold may move without being imported or exported.) Many overlooked this fact, as did Oskar Morgenstern in his monumental work, *International Financial Transactions and Business Cycles*. Chapter 5 of Morgenstern's book is given over almost entirely to a discussion of supposed "violations" of the gold points.[16] Gold points are usually calculated by taking the statutory price of gold and estimating shipping costs between gold centers. Ideally, such a calculation would have meaning, but in a world where central banks manipulate gold prices, it is not surprising that gold points calculated in this manner would be violated. The true gold points would have to be refigured

16. Oskar Morgenstern, *International Financial Transactions and Business Cycles* (Princeton: Princeton University Press for NBER, 1959).

each time a central bank changed its buying price for gold. Gold points calculated in this manner would never be violated —arbitrage would make sure of that.

One might now ask if the Bank of England observes the rules of the game. Before the twentieth century, bank rate changes were often ineffective. After 1900 their effectiveness increased until the governor could make his unequivocal statement to the National Monetary Commission in 1910. Gold operations probably reached their height under the governorship of Lidderdale in 1890 and 1891, but were used extensively enough during later periods to make gold point calculations difficult. The evolution of policy tools is reflected here, for Morgenstern found few violations after 1900, with the exception of Paris-London, which was a special case because of French bimetalism. Later violations also occurred for London-Berlin exchanges but after 1893, violations were all on the side of Berlin. The Reichsbank could protect its reserve by requiring all gold to be obtained at the main office in Berlin, thus raising shipping costs for gold exporters outside Berlin.

The Bank of England quite obviously used other policy tools, in particular various operations on the gold market, either to supplement bank rate policy or to replace it. Again there is the question of whether or not the Bank of England really observed the rules of the game.

Evidence suggests that Bank of England operations were not the passive sort predicted by the rules of the game and also that policy actions were asymmetrical; the bank was willing and able to take precautionary action regarding its reserve and the situation of English internal trade. The following can be considered a concise statement of the rules of the game of the international gold standard: The bank rate is raised when gold is flowing out of the country in order to protect the reserve and lowered when an excess of gold has been imported into the country. As a contrast, we have the interview of the Governor of the Bank of England with the National Monetary Commission. "The bank rate is raised with the object either of preventing gold from leaving the country, or of attracting gold to the country, and lowered when it is completely out of touch with the market rate and circumstances do not render it necessary to induce import of gold."[17] Notice how little resemblance this position bears to the rules of the game. The governor of the Bank of England was willing to admit that bank rate should be raised when gold was flowing out of the country, the action which the rules suggest (in practice the bank often tried to avoid this policy), but when there was a surplus of gold or an inflow, the governor was unwilling to suggest the opposite policy. The operation of the gold standard requires that central banks react to both outflows and inflows.

Any type of discretionary action on the part of the bank was also forbidden by the rules of the game, but again there is evidence that such action was often taken to protect the reserve. In 1890, when economic and political troubles were brewing in South America, the bank raised its rate of discount. By July, bank rate stood at 4 percent and the outflow of gold had been stopped. The bank, however, did not feel its reserve was large enough, so it raised bank rate to 5 percent. Sayers comments, "At a time when gold was actually flowing in inappreciable quantities the rise to five percent took the market by surprise, but was approved by the *Economist* as a 'wise measure of precaution.' "[18]

While convertibility may have been the main concern of the Bank of England, there is no doubt that the bank also paid attention to the condition of English internal trade. The bank was very sensitive to charges by businessmen that interest rates

17. U.S. National Monetary Commission, p. 29.
18. Sayers, *Bank of England Operations*, p. 119.

were often unnecessarily changed in response to remote conditions. This situation contrasted with that of the Bank of France, whose discount rate was constant for long periods of time. However, France's bimetalism gave the Bank of France a second method of contending with any strain on its reserve, since it could redeem notes in silver if it wished.

Bank of England operations on the gold market seem to have been one way of easing the strain on internal trade caused by frequent changes in bank rate. Consider this quotation from the *Economist*:

And in a time of gold scarcity, such as that through which we have been passing, it is certainly much better for the trade of the country, and probably better on the whole, for the Bank also, that it should seek to attract gold by raising the price of gold coin, than by raising its rate of discount. Both measures may be necessary, but certainly the former is less disturbing to business than the latter, and is not unlikely to be less costly to the bank itself than the efforts it has to make to lift the market rates up nearer to its own level.[19]

The Bank of England had a difficult time operating on the gold standard; the Federal Reserve might have found it much more difficult, as the world gold market at the time was in London, not New York. After World War I, the Federal Reserve did find itself unwilling to follow the rules of the game—witness gold "sterilization" operations. Such operations —taken to neutralize the effects of gold inflows—indicate most clearly the difficulty central banks have always encountered when on the gold standard.

Conclusion

There clearly is a connection between the real bills doctrine and the gold standard. The real bills doctrine was the means

19. *Economist*, Feb. 14, 1885, p. 186.

by which the money supply was to be adjusted in composition and quantity to the requirements of the domestic economy. The creation and discount of real bills represent loans from purchasers to sellers by way of the banking system. The degree to which the banking system will grant such loans, thereby increasing the money supply, will depend on the state of the market for money and credit. However, this market depends on the state of the foreign exchanges if the economy is on the gold standard. An adverse movement in foreign exchanges could occur at the same time the domestic economy was expanding. A domestic expansion could even be the cause of an adverse movement in the exchanges: rising domestic prices could increase imports and decrease exports. The rules of the game would call for an increase in the central bank rate of discount to protect the reserve.

Many of the supporters of the real bills theory seem to have ignored the effects of higher interest rates on the discounting procedure, or at least failed to carry through this line of reasoning to discover the ultimate relationship between the two doctrines. For example, consider the statement by H. Parker Willis that one of the two basic principles of the Federal Reserve Act was that there should be "no commercial transaction that cannot obtain a note issue to facilitate it."[20]

It was probable that if the monetary authority attempted to adhere to the gold standard and the real bills doctrine, it would find the two policy guides in conflict. If the authorities raised the rate of discount and reduced either the money supply or its rate of growth, some discounts which would have been made at the old rates will not be made at the new, higher rates. In other words there might now be some commercial transactions which would not yield notes that could profitably be

20. Willis, The Federal Reserve, p. 254.

discounted. This is exactly the problem encountered by the Bank of England: should domestic or international considerations determine policy? It was difficult for the Bank of England, located in the world's premier money market to achieve its desired ends. How much more difficult would it have been for the newly created Federal Reserve System?

The theoretical bases of the Federal Reserve Act were two economic myths. One was an outmoded system of finance which the American economy had discarded three decades before. The other was an idealized version of the international gold standard which was widely accepted for many decades even though it probably never existed. Attempts during the early years of the Federal Reserve to reestablish the gold standard and to create a commercial bill market were doomed to failure. This was not because World War I caused profound changes in economic relations, but because conditions had changed long before. Had the Federal Reserve been based on a clearer understanding of economic arrangements, theoretical and operational development might have proceeded at a much faster rate after the war.

CHAPTER 9

The Development of Federal Reserve Theory, 1914–1923

The Federal Reserve System was hailed as a new beginning for banking in the United States, but its supposedly firm foundation was built on sand. This chapter is concerned with the operational changes which occurred during the first ten years, and Chapter 10 deals with the changes which were necessary to improve the system's organization. These changes came about as experience showed that the system had a choice regarding its development: it could be the passive "lender of last resort" found in the strict language (and perhaps the intent) of the Federal Reserve Act, or it could become a dynamic institution for economic control. The system became the latter, while often proclaiming itself the former.

The choice may not have been made consciously at first, but the activities of the Federal Reserve during World War I demonstrated that the power of the system to affect economic variables was immense. In terms of development the war was a major determining force. The effects of the European war were felt, long before the United States entered the conflict, when the system had hardly begun to form. Wartime exigencies turned the Federal Reserve away from its intended function of dealing in real bills, but this result was not unexpected. In times of war, central banks historically have been more or less the captives of government policy. This captivity continued after World War I ended—until the government had satisfied itself about its own finances. The next few years were spent finding both a clear understanding of the system's mission and developing policy tools for carrying out that mission.

This chapter discusses the Federal Reserve System's early years from the perspective of the preceding chapters. The system was a product of nineteenth-century financial problems and the reform movement which resulted. The structure and purpose of the Federal Reserve System were profoundly affected by the American financial experience.

Many studies deal with the early years of the Federal Reserve System,[1] but they seldom begin from the point of view developed here. Most often, they compare the system's early years with central banking theory developed during and after this period. Because these other studies offer detailed analyses of system policies and their effects; this chapter concentrates on broad policy matters and the philosophy behind them.

1. The best known of these studies are W. R. Burgess, *The Reserve Banks and the Money Market* (New York: Harper, 1927); Lester V. Chandler, *Benjamin Strong, Central Banker* (Washington, D.C.: The Brookings Institution, 1958); C. O. Hardy, *Credit Policies of the Federal Reserve System* (Washington, D.C.: The Brookings Institution, 1932); H. L. Reed, *Federal Reserve Policy, 1921–1930* (New York: McGraw-Hill, 1930); Winfield W. Riefler, *Money Rates and Money Markets in the United States* (New York: Harper, 1930) and Wicker, *Federal Reserve Policy.* Also very helpful is Milton Friedman and Anna Schwartz, *A Monetary History of the United States, 1867–1960* (Princeton: Princeton University Press, 1963), chaps. 4, 5, and 6. A recent study is the report of the Banking and Currency Committee of the House of Representatives entitled *Federal Reserve Structure and the Development of Federal Reserve Policy: 1915–1935,* Staff Report of the Subcommittee on Domestic Finance, Committee on Banking and Currency (Washington, D.C.: GPO, 1971). The latter, while making some attempt to recognize the Federal Reserve's historical antecedents, falls lamentably short of a correct interpretation of the system's milieu.

The Question of Approach

A recurring problem in the study of economic history and the history of economic thought is the relationship between general economic conditions and the economic thought of any period.[2] What was the impact of events in any particular period upon contemporary economic literature? There is also the problem of "the quality of their (contemporary economists) intellectual response, as judged by the standards of later times."[3] This problem is particularly important in discussions of the early development of the Federal Reserve System because options open to policy makers today did not exist then.

A discussion of the real bills doctrine must first determine what banking theory lies behind any advocacy of the discount of real bills and, second, establish whether the theory was a correct one. Some writers, Mints for example, do not take the first step and consider the matter of theory. This approach is unfortunate, since widely differing views are often lumped together. Warburg and Willis are put in the same category, even though from a theoretical standpoint Willis's views were more objectionable than Warburg's views. Schumpeter's view of banking policy is relevant here.[4] Virtually every modern criticism of early Federal Reserve policy pays little or no attention to the fact that few policy makers advocated the "objectionable"

2. This is an oft-debated subject. See, for instance, the exchange between A. W. Coats and William R. Allen in "The Interpretation of Mercantilist Economics: Some Historiographical Problems," *History of Political Economy*, 5 (Fall 1973), 485–498. Joseph Schumpeter, in his monumental work *The History of Economic Analysis*, pays a great deal of attention to the political and social backgrounds of the periods into which he divides the history of economic analysis. These cultural conditions define both the problems and the acceptable ground rules for their solution.

3. Coats and Allen, "The Interpretation of Mercantilist Economics," p. 486.

4. See above, Chapter 7.

version of the real bills theory. In their public statements policy makers did not say that the proper volume of credit would be maintained if only real bills were discounted, but rather that the purpose of the agency which they served was to accommodate industry and trade. Furthermore, they demonstrated by their actions that they believed other tools were necessary if credit was to be kept within reasonable bounds.

The statements of purpose and policy reflected the options open to policy makers at the time, and it is unjust to criticize early policy because it was not based on the theory and tools available to modern central bankers. Indeed, the early period of the system represents the developmental stage of the theory and tools which exist today.

The Rapidly Changing World

The world into which the Federal Reserve System emerged was far different from the one for which the act was designed. The act's preamble gives some indication of the expected use of the system. The system's purpose was to provide a response to the periodic crises which had plagued the American financial sector. While there were many contributing causes, and none of the crises between 1873 and 1907 were exactly alike, one of the major characteristics of the American financial sector was its susceptability to exogenous shocks because of the lack of a centralized reserve, and a central authority to direct policy. This point was particularly important since the United States was a debtor nation on international account. Each summer American banks would go into debt to British bankers to the amount of about $500 million on short-term loans which would be paid off as crops were shipped in the autumn.[5] Any

5. See Federal Reserve Board, *First Annual Report of the Federal Reserve Board* (Washington, D.C.: GPO, 1915), p. 13; Chandler, *Benjamin Strong*, p. 55; Benjamin Haggot Beckhart, *Federal Reserve System* (New York: American Institute of Banking, 1972), p. 135.

bottlenecks in this process had serious repercussions on the American financial scene.

With the outbreak of war in Europe in the summer of 1914, this process of foreign financing of American trade was impeded. Hostilities decreased exports very rapidly because German ships were withdrawn from American trade, and British shipping service was disrupted by the outbreak of fighting. The result was a desperate scramble by European investors to liquidate their American holdings. The sterling exchange rate rose, and an outflow of gold to Europe followed as American borrowings were liquidated. As in previous crises, people lost confidence in the banks and attempted to withdraw their deposits.

This financial uncertainty occurred before the reserve banks could be organized and opened for business. Fortunately, Congress had extended the Aldrich-Vreeland Act, and the first and last issue of Aldrich-Vreeland emergency currency took place in the autumn of 1914. This issue served its purpose, allowing the transfer of bank deposits into bank notes and avoiding widespread suspension.

After 1914 events began to move in the other direction. Preoccupation with war production necessitated large imports of American goods by the allied powers. The premium on sterling rapidly disappeared, and the Allies faced the problem of acquiring dollars with which to pay for their imports from the United States. A large part of the short-term debt which had recently been an onus for America's creditors was rapidly liquidated to pay for goods bought from American producers.

During the war's later stages, the Allies exported gold to the United States and floated loans from American concerns to pay for their purchases. Between 1914 and 1917, the United States gold stock increased by $1 billion. By 1917 the United States held one third of the world's monetary gold stock. The financial transactions caused by the war rapidly transformed America from a debtor on the international scene to a substantial creditor.

World War I also marked another important change in international financial relations. This change, the demise of the international gold standard, went hand-in-hand with the emergence of the United States as a substantial creditor on international account. The heretofore unknown fragility of nineteenth-century economic and political relationships was shatteringly demonstrated. After 1914 the gold standard as it previously existed was gone forever. The continual attempts to resurrect the prewar monetary system and the resulting apotheosis of the gold standard, reflected the commonly held desire to regain the lost concreteness of prewar financial relations. Since the Federal Reserve Act was designed to work within the international gold standard,[6] this change was one more difficulty for policy makers.

It is probably fortunate that the reserve banks were not formed at the time of the monetary stringency in the autumn of 1914. Their resources would necessarily have been very small and they might not have survived the pressure. By the time the reserve banks opened for business on November 16, 1914, the worst of the crisis was over, and the reserve banks entered into a financial sector which was relatively stable.

The combination of changing economic conditions and the establishment of the Federal Reserve System eventually resulted in American financial pre-eminence; New York began to displace London as the major world credit market. This process

6. In the standard provision dealing with inconsistencies between the Federal Reserve Act and other legislations (section 26), the Gold Standard Act is specifically exempted from the blanket repeal. The inconsistency between the act's discounting provisions and the theoretical working of the gold standard has already been noted.

made the Federal Reserve System's capacity to influence national and world financial activity all the greater, and increased the responsibilities of the system.

Experience and the Development of Federal Reserve Policy

Federal Reserve policy, at least as it was reflected in the system's actions over the first ten years, was often constrained by exogenous forces. The decade divides rather easily into three distinct periods: November 16, 1914, until the declaration of war on April 2, 1917; the war period (including the postwar financing years); and the period from late 1919 until the end of 1923 and the famous *Tenth Annual Report.*

The preceding chapters have suggested the role of the Federal Reserve System as foreseen by those who were closest to it. For Willis and Glass, the act was the legislation of the real bills doctrine, reflecting the belief that by limiting the system's discounts and open market purchases to "real bills," credit would be properly controlled. It is extremely difficult, if not impossible, to find evidence that Federal Reserve Board members or other important policy makers accepted this strict version of the real bills doctrine. (Of course, Glass as secretary of the treasury was an ex officio member of the board.) Despite this fact, the Federal Reserve System (both the board and the banks) has been criticized for its alleged adherence to the real bills doctrine.[7] There are two reasons for this paradox. First there is the common omission by most authors of any clear definition of the real bills theory. Unless it is known exactly what is meant by the term "real bills," one cannot assess policy statements and their underlying theory; this point has been demonstrated before, and is asserted even more sharply in this chapter. The inability or unwillingness of some

7. See particularly House Report, *Federal Reserve Structure and the Development of Federal Reserve Policy: 1915–1935.*

authors to view the new Federal Reserve System properly, with respect to what it was and when it was, presents another problem.

A further complication is that there were at least two possible loci of power in the system and they were in competition. The problems caused by the structure of the act itself will be discussed later, but other structural problems arose from actual operations. The main difficulty was that the board and the banks occupied different positions with regard to actual operation in the money market. Ideally the board was charged with the oversight of broad policy questions, and the day-to-day implementation of policy was left to the reserve banks. Under the divisional system supposedly established by the Federal Reserve Act, questions regarding organization of a national credit policy, or even whether the act intended that such a policy should exist, were left unanswered. The necessity for a nationwide view existed and was met by the governors of the individual banks or by the board, depending upon specific circumstances and the power of various individuals.

During this period Benjamin Strong was the most knowledgeable authority on matters of money and credit. Although Strong's influence on policy was immense during the first decade, the board may have acceded for all the wrong reasons. Even when there was substantial agreement between the banks and the board,[8] consensus was often reached via two different routes.

8. It should not be forgotten that neither group was unanimous. Strong was often challenged by other governors, particularly those in Chicago and Boston. See Chandler, *Benjamin Strong, passim.* Likewise, the board was seldom one voice on policy questions. The board in particular was subject to much switching of views (and votes), a circumstance which indicates either the lack of a strong theoretical foundation or, just as likely, political pressure.

The First Period, 1914–1917

During its early years the Federal Reserve System was relatively powerless to influence monetary conditions. The new reserve banks had small or nearly nonexistent portfolios. A central banking system can have little effect on monetary conditions if it is not in the market. When money is so easy that commercial banks can expand the money supply without facing the necessity of borrowing (rediscounting) to replenish their reserves, the powers of a central banking system are greatly reduced.

The Federal Reserve System and its member banks found themselves in just such a situation in 1914 and 1915. The decrease in reserve requirements under the Federal Reserve Act enhanced the ability of the member banks to lend, and the reserve banks had no means by which they could force restraint upon the credit expansion. In addition there was the large gold inflow, over $1 billion during the neutrality period, which also increased bank reserves. The system did succeed in convincing member banks to make their initial reserve deposits largely in gold or gold certificates instead of the combination of lawful money and commercial paper allowed by the law. Had banks deposited reserves in the form of commercial paper, their capacity for expansion would have been much greater. The situation was what would be expected in an economy operating near full employment. The large gold inflow and the increase in reserves contributed to a rapid rise in the price level.[9]

For the most part this first period was a time of organization. Technical questions such as check clearing, eligibility requirements, and other matters occupied most of the system's time and attention. System officials made policy statements, but

9. For a more detailed discussion of the changes in economic indicators during this period, see Milton Friedman and Anna J. Schwartz, *A Monetary History of the United States*, chap. 5.

there was little opportunity for action. Nevertheless, their views should be discussed.

When the Federal Reserve Act was passed, many believed that the system's primary function was to provide aid during emergencies. In fact, a strict interpretation of the act leaves one with this view, but the Federal Reserve Board quickly rejected this notion. The *First Annual Report* states that the "duty [of the reserve banks] plainly is not to await emergencies but by anticipation, to do what it can to prevent them."[10] The *Report* went on to say:

The more complete adaptation of the credit mechanism and facilities of the country to the needs of industry, commerce, and agriculture—with all their seasonal fluctuations and contingencies—should be the constant aim of a Reserve Bank's management. To provide and maintain a fluid condition of credit, such as will make of the Reserve Banks at all times and under all conditions institutions of accommodation *in the larger and public sense of the term* is the first responsibility of a Reserve Bank.[11]

One might wonder what the board meant by the last phrase. Were reserve banks to meet all demands for accommodation, or was it possible that at times accommodations should be curtailed? The question was answered when the board maintained that there "will be times when the great weight of their influence should be exerted to secure a freer extension of credit and an easing of rates. . . . There will just as certainly, however be other times when prudence and a proper regard for the common good will require that an opposite course should be pursued and accommodations curtailed."[12]

Obviously, the Federal Reserve Board anticipated circumstances (it was certainly not difficult to do so) which would

10. Federal Reserve Board, *First Annual Report*, pp. 17–19.
11. Ibid., emphasis added.
12. Ibid., p. 18.

require that credit be tightened even if paper offered was eligible for discount. Some even argued that besides raising the discount rate, making discounts more dear, the reserve banks could refuse to discount eligible paper altogether. The unpalatable practice of refusing discounts could be avoided if the reserve banks sold government securities at the same time they discounted commercial paper, but this practice was not free from problems either.

The idea that the reserve banks were to operate only during times of emergency was never held by the system; the board at once took a larger view of its responsibilities, but the conception of the Federal Reserve as an emergency institution did have its impact. For instance, some felt that this view had produced troublesome features in the act. E. A. Goldenweiser, later the board's chief economic adviser during the critical 1930's, apparently thought so. Reflecting back on the establishment of the Federal Reserve, he maintained that the "definition of the kind of paper that the Federal Reserve banks could discount was determined by this conception of the functions of the Federal Reserve banks [to act as emergency institutions], which is narrow even when viewed apart from the more general central banking duties of the banks."[13] While this opinion is not the whole story behind the law's eligibility requirements, it does allow a clearer understanding of those provisions. Goldenweiser also indicates that insiders knew from the beginning that their actions might be contrary to the spirit of the act. Evidence suggests that Willis—and there were probably others among the early supporters of the bill—did not conceive of the system as merely an emergency organization. But sup-

13. E. A. Goldenweiser, "Significance of the Lending Functions of the Federal Reserve Banks," paper read before the annual meetings of the American Statistical Association, Dec. 30, 1935, p. 1, copy in the Library of the Board of Governors of the Federal Reserve System.

porters of the act in Congress might not have gone so far as to advocate outright monetary and credit control by the system. Willis's view probably lay somewhere between the conception of the system as strictly an emergency institution and an organization for active control of money and credit.

Despite the belief of Federal Reserve policy makers that their mandate went beyond the strict language of the act, they had little or no quarrel with the act's eligibility requirements. For the most part, Federal Reserve officials accepted the requirements wholeheartedly. System officials often argued that their legislative mandate was to deal in real bills. C. S. Hamlin, first governor of the Federal Reserve Board, maintained that two of the act's basic principles were "that commercial paper must be turned from the non-liquid investment into a quick liquid asset; that commercial paper based upon the trade and commerce of the people is the best self-liquidating asset that can be had."[14]

In 1916, W. P. G. Harding, second governor of the Federal Reserve Board, remarked: "It is clear that the intent of the Act is to safeguard the self-liquidating character of acceptances, as securities of an investment nature are barred, and provision is made that the transaction should be based upon either an actual sale of goods or upon the conveyance of legal title to goods which can be readily marketed."[15]

Therefore, while the Federal Reserve Board rejected any

14. C. S. Hamlin, "The Federal Reserve Established and in Operation," an address delivered before the New York Chamber of Commerce, Dec. 3, 1914, p. 7. A copy of this address is in the Library of the Board of Governors of the Federal Reserve System.

15. W. P. G. Harding, "The Present Position and the Future Development of the Federal Reserve System," an address before the Forum of the New York Chapter of the American Institute of Banking, Nov. 1, 1916, p. 10. A copy of this address is in the Library of the Board of Governors of the Federal Reserve System.

literal interpretation of the act which would have limited the system to a passive role, it did tend to accept the act's eligibility requirements. This was certainly true in the beginning, although this position may have been modified later. Clearly this agreement on eligibility existed because the main concern was to allow credit for so-called legitimate uses, while at the same time limiting credit for speculative purposes.

The Federal Reserve Act was to achieve this purpose by making investments in real bills more attractive. These investments were presumably made superior to the standard speculative loan—call loans on the New York Stock Exchange—because only nonspeculative loans could be discounted by the Federal Reserve System. Prior to the Federal Reserve Act the banking system's main reliance for secondary reserves was placed on call loans. If another type of investment, real bills, was made as liquid as call loans, it was believed that funds which had formerly been placed in the call loan market would be invested in commercial paper, thus limiting the speculative use of funds. By limiting Federal Reserve discounts to commercial paper, it was asserted that Federal Reserve credit would find only productive uses.

At the same time that the board stressed the virtues of commercial paper, Benjamin Strong, through the New York Bank, was attempting to create an open market for such paper. Strong concentrated on developing the use of bankers' acceptances, which were newly allowed under the Federal Reserve Act. Strong's desire for such a market did not stem from a belief that development of real bills as a bank asset would help control speculation. His intention was rather to create an environment in which the Federal Reserve System could exercise monetary management.[16] Strong realized that for the system to exercise power over money and credit, an open market in

16. See Chandler, *Benjamin Strong*, chap. 3, pt. II.

negotiable securities must exist. Bankers' acceptances in foreign trade were one of the means by which the Bank of England had influenced the London money market and managed the gold standard for the previous third of a century.

These matters were the primary occupations of the system during the first period. An environment was created in which the Federal Reserve System could act, not by passive participation, but by direct action. The banks and the board also attempted to find a common ground for action. These goals were achieved in part, although regarding common theoretical grounds it was an achievement more of appearance than of substance. The system's actual operations were few, taken with an eye more toward income than to broad monetary policy. All the initial planning suddenly became irrelevant when the United States joined the world at war.

The Years of Captivity, 1917–1919

After the United States entered the war, the situation of the Federal Reserve changed very rapidly, but not in a way which gave the system any power to act independently. In the previous period the system's inability to act was due to its newness and consequent lack of resources with which to affect the money markets. In the second period, from 1917 to 1919, its inability to act independently was caused by subordination to the war efforts of the Treasury Department.

During the war the main source of government funds was the sale of government securities. While the long-term bond issues, the Liberty Loans, and the Victory Loan are better known, the government also sold shorter maturities. These were primarily certificates of indebtedness and Treasury notes. Since the Federal Reserve Act made all government securities, as well as real bills, eligible as security for Federal Reserve loans, the spectrum of possible Federal Reserve loan collateral was widened substantially.

The Treasury wanted the system to discriminate in favor of loans backed by government securities by allowing them lower discount rates. As a result, government securities became very important as collateral for Federal Reserve loans. Although the reserve banks did agree to take a $50 million issue of ninety-day certificates of indebtedness, for the most part, the banks adamantly resisted Treasury attempts to burden them with a large amount of government debt. This position did not prevent the reserve banks from purchasing bonds on the open market or from member banks. What was really at issue was the Federal Reserve's reluctance to purchase securities directly from the Treasury because of the financial abuses which might possibly result.

Resistance to direct purchases meant that the main vehicle of the system's support for government finance was the discounting of member banks' own notes, which were backed primarily by government securities. The reserve banks did not own the debt but allowed commercial banks to carry it from the government to the people. This practice was allowed by an amendment to the Federal Reserve Act passed in 1916 which permitted member banks to borrow on their own fifteen-day notes, using eligible securities as collateral. Such a provision originally had been placed in the act by the Senate, but rejected by the House. The practice was widespread during the war and continued during peace time.

As a result of the war effort and the discrimination in favor of loans backed by government securities, the great majority of Federal Reserve credit was based on security other than real bills. In April 1917, when the United States entered the war, no Federal Reserve discounts were backed by government securities. By May 1918, 81.2 percent of Federal Reserve purchases were commercial paper (the sum of member banks' rediscounts and open market purchases) backed by government securities.[17] Federal Reserve credit backed by government debt reached a high point of 95.2 percent in May 1919 and continued at high levels through 1923, never falling below 46 percent. This aspect of what was called commercial paper is easily seen in Charts 9.1 and 9.2.[18]

Similarly, Federal Reserve purchases of government securities increased rapidly from 1917 until 1919. In April 1917, such purchases amounted to only $4.37 million, or 4.3 percent of total investments. In March 1918, Federal Reserve Bank purchases of government securities amounted to over $1,099 million, or 55.1 percent of total investments. From May 1917 through June 1918 the average monthly purchases of government securities were roughly twice the average monthly amount of acceptances purchased in the open market. While purchases of government securities after this period continued to grow in absolute amounts, they suffered a relative decline.

Not all of the credit extended from 1917 to 1919 based on government debt was used to carry that debt between the government and the ultimate investors. Many banks simply used loans of this kind to obtain funds for regular use. The lower discount rate offered on this paper made it more profitable for member banks to hold their commercial paper and use their government securities as loan collateral. As a result, commercial paper virtually disappeared from the portfolios of the reserve banks.

17. See Charts 9.1–9.3 for more information on Federal Reserve investments discussed in this chapter.

18. Chart 9.2 reveals that virtually all the variation in total commercial paper comes from variations in the portion backed by government obligations. A close look at Chart 9.1 reveals that the level of outstanding commercial paper not backed by government obligations, real commercial paper, is a relatively constant amount. This opens up many possible speculations about member bank use of the discount window.

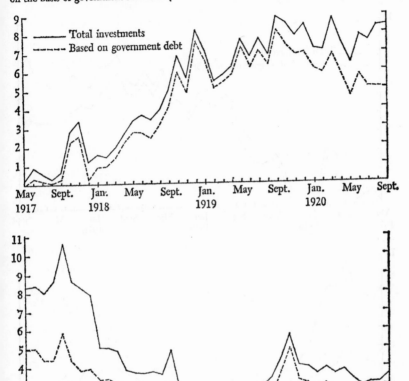

Chart 9.1. Total Federal Reserve investment operations and the amount extended on the basis of government securities (in millions of dollars), 1917–1923.

Charts 9.1–9.3 were constructed from tables in the *Annual Reports* of the Federal Reserve Board, 1916–1923. These data represent the flow of Federal Reserve investments rather than the stock of investments at any one time, for the former better represent the changes in Federal Reserve operations. Chart 9.1 shows the increasing dependence of Federal Reserve credit on government obligations, whether issued directly for the purchase of government securities, or indirectly where government obligations were used as collateral for member bank loans. Chart 9.2 shows the total amount of "commercial" paper and the amount of "commercial" paper which had government obligations as collateral. Chart 9.3 compares the relative magnitudes of commercial paper bought in the open market and government securities purchased by the system.

Chart 9.2.   Total commercial paper and commercial paper backed by government securities (in millions of dollars), 1917–1923.

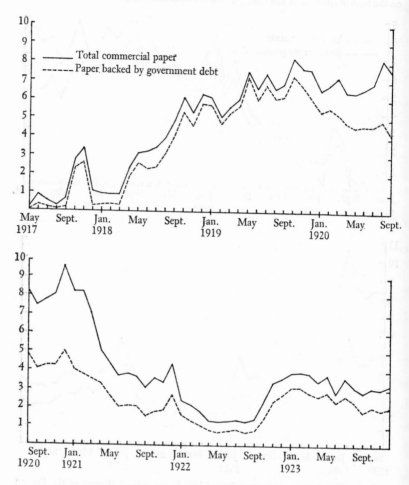

The period of captivity continued throughout the war, through the subsequent postwar financing, and even through some refunding operations in the autumn of 1919. During this period the system's discount rates were kept low in order that government loans might be placed at low interest rates. The Treasury was concerned about two factors: the additional cost

Chart 9.3. Open market paper and government securities purchased (in thousands of dollars), 1921–1923.

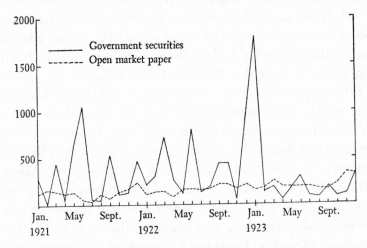

to the government and ultimately to the people that higher interest rates would entail; and the consequent devaluation of earlier issues which would occur if later bond issues were placed at higher interest rates. The government was understandably reluctant to have this happen. Both of these considerations were primarily political.

These political choices were not without their economic effects. Most of the government expenditures financed by bond issues handled through the banking system were not offset by savings in other sectors. Purchases of bonds were not equivalent to savings; instead they were based on extensions of credit by the banking system. Hence, there was inflation. Inflation was possible as long as the banking system acted as an intermediary between the government and the final purchasers of the bonds. The reserves obtained through the discounts used to carry bonds could maintain other loans as well. The loans made to provide for the purchase of the bonds required only a fraction of the value of the bonds as reserves.

Two characteristics of this period are more important than the overall economic impact of World War I: the creation of a substantial amount of government debt, both long term and short term; and the precedent set during this period when a substantial amount of Federal Reserve credit came to be based on government debt, either directly or indirectly. Expansion of the supply of short-term government securities together with the market which resulted from their sale created an almost ideal field of operations for the reserve banks. Today, short-term government debt is the only area in which the Federal Reserve engages in substantial open market operations, but before World War I there was no market for short-term government securities. Today there is no longer a market for the type of commercial paper once purchased by the system. The importance of such a change can be completely understood only in the context of the economic thought of the time.

The emergence of federal government securities as collateral made the system's portfolio more flexible. The accommodation of business, industry, and agriculture was still the Federal Reserve's primary concern, but transactions in areas other than real bills no longer bore the stigma of previous years. This increased flexibility, combined with the view that the system had some responsibility to oversee the market for Treasury certificates, widened the field of Federal Reserve operations. The narrow conception of the Federal Reserve Act had disappeared forever.

In terms of Federal Reserve policy these two developments were the most important legacy of World War I. The Federal Reserve System had established the precedent of dealing in government debt, and a large market for that debt had been created in which policy measures could have an effect through operations on the open market.

On Its Own, 1919–1923

After December 1919, when the Treasury and the Federal Reserve Board finally assented to a rise in reserve bank discount rates, the Federal Reserve System was able to go beyond merely advising on policy matters. The system could now formulate and act upon its own views of the monetary and banking system. This does not mean that there was unanimity in the system. Indeed, there continued to be disputes over policy, just as there were disputes over the locus of power. In this period, late 1919 through 1923, the Federal Reserve attempted to determine its role in the American economy. First, there was the matter of determining the system's mission and, second, determining the best way to carry out that mission.

After a slowdown in the economy at the war's end, prices and output had begun to swing upward again, supported by the Federal Reserve System's easy money policies. The individual reserve banks requested discount rates increases throughout most of 1919, but these were opposed by the Treasury and thus, the Federal Reserve Board. The system's policy makers were aware of the effects of Federal Reserve policy. The problem was pressure from outside the system; mainly from the executive branch. At that time the board was still extremely susceptible to political pressure, and the wartime Overman Act could have been used to strip the board of all its power if it refused to go along with government policy. Even without such pressure, the board might not have acted any differently. If the *Annual Report* for 1919 gives any indication of the board's views, one must conclude that it believed that a rise in the discount rate would be very harmful to the Treasury's funding actions.[19]

19. *Sixth Annual Report of the Federal Reserve Board* (Washington, D.C.: GPO, 1920), p. 3.

Late in 1919 discount rates were raised after the Treasury finally withdrew its objections to higher rates. Some officials believed that the time for increased rates had passed, and that they would now be harmful; this belief may have been correct. The monetary policies of 1919 and 1920—easy money and then restriction—were followed by the crash of 1920–1921.[20] The Federal Reserve was later blamed for not taking proper action in 1919 to halt the expansion before it got out of hand. To the extent that monetary policy was involved in the 1920–1921 crash, the real blame lies not with the Federal Reserve System (certainly not with the reserve banks) but with the Treasury and its insistence on low discount rates to aid government funding operations. In the case of the board, which was in a position to arbitrate, two facts should be noted: first, some members were honestly mistaken about the efficacy of certain policies; second, it appears that the board was unable to overcome Treasury domination, and so failed to take necessary action.[21]

Nevertheless, this period allowed the system ample opportunity to inspect its tools and the theory behind them. Unfortunately, the inspection was not always perceptive, and much of the lesson learned was lost, only to be relearned in 1929 and 1930. From 1919 until 1923 incontrovertible evidence emerged which should have put the strong version of the real bills doctrine to rest forever, at least as far as the Federal Reserve System was concerned. Unfortunately, there was no uniformity in the effects of the lesson within the system. The reserve banks, particularly in New York, learned it better than did the board. As we shall see, though Benjamin Strong and

20. See Friedman and Schwartz, *Monetary History of the United States, 1867–1960*, pp. 221–239. In terms of severity, but not length, this crash was the worst in the twentieth century and perhaps in the entire history of the United States.

21. *Sixth Annual Report*, pp. 1–3.

others had freed themselves completely from the shackles of the real bills theory, its influence, while weakened, was still important in many quarters. The declining influence of the real bills theory and the realization that new tools were needed are related, since both factors deal with the difference between qualitative and quantitative control, a distinction stressed in the *Tenth Annual Report*.

The section of the *Tenth Annual Report* which discussed the guides to credit policy states that the "Board is fully aware of the fact that the problem of credit extension involves the question of amount or volume as well as the question of kind or character; otherwise stated, involves a quantitative as well as a qualitative determination."[22] This statement by itself reads much like a partial renunciation of the strict version of the real bills doctrine. The board professed its belief that it was not enough to decide on credit applications by eligibility requirements alone, and that a further policy guide was needed.

One of the primary reasons for this change in attitude was the crisis of 1920–1921. The preceding period of speculative price increases was not caused by overinvestment in securities, but by overinvestment in inventories. Retailers placed orders with many different producers and wholesalers, knowing that their orders could not all be met, but desiring to ensure that their future stocks would be adequate. In many cases goods were held in anticipation of price increases.[23] Much of this speculation, especially in inventory holdings, was financed by bank credit granted on real bills, that is, bills drawn on goods in the process of distribution. While such inventory specula-

22. *Tenth Annual Report of the Federal Reserve System* (Washington, D.C.: GPO, 1924), pp. 29–39.
23. For a more complete view of this process see George Soule, *Prosperity Decade from War to Depression: 1917–1929* (New York: Holt, Rinehart and Winston, 1964), chap. 4.

tion certainly was not the sort of process envisaged by those who believed in the strict version of the real bills doctrine, the bills were virtually indistinguishable from ordinary commercial bills. It rapidly became apparent that "real" bills could be drawn in support of speculation, just as easily as personal notes.

This fact was noted by board members. In 1920, Adolph C. Miller, an economist and one of the original board members, stated in an article for the London Times, "In the opinion of many, however, the existing credit situation . . . which calls for correction is not alone the excessive use of credit in speculation, but the excessive use of credit in ordinary trade and industry. The inflations produced by the war have given a speculative tinge to much ordinary business and industrial enterprise."[24] In the same vein, W. P. G. Harding, later in the same year maintained that "the fact must be realized that however desirable on general principles continued expansion of trade and industry may be, such developments must accommodate themselves to the actual supply of capital and credit available."[25] This statement of Harding's, when compared to some of his earlier comments,[26] shows the development of the views of some board members.

The system's experience in 1919–1920 caused doubts among board members concerning the correctness of the real bills doctrine, at least in the version held by Willis and Laughlin. The board was not able to throw off all vestiges of the doctrine,

24. Adolph C. Miller, "American Banking: Control of the Credit System," printed in the London Times Annual Financial and Commercial Review, Jan. 23, 1920, p. 11. A copy of this article is in the Library of the Board of Governors of the Federal Reserve System.

25. W. P. G. Harding, "The Functions and Policies of the Federal Reserve Board," address before the Chamber of Commerce of Cleveland, Ohio, Sept. 16, 1920, pp. 6–7. A copy is in the Library of the Board of Governors of the Federal Reserve System.

26. See page 184 above.

however. In the very same paragraph as the quotation given above concerning quantitative measures, the *Tenth Annual Report* went on to say:

It is the view of the Board that it is not necessary to go outside of the Federal Reserve Act to find suitable methods of estimating the adjustment of the volume of credit provided by the Federal reserve banks to the volume of credit needs. . . . The provisions of this act already quoted indicate that the needs for credit which are recognized by the act as appropriate are those derived from agriculture, industry and trade. It is the belief of the board that there will be little danger that the credit created and contributed by the Federal reserve banks will be in excessive volume if restricted to productive uses.[27]

The contradiction between this statement and the earlier one is more apparent than real. The board was attempting to resurrect the automaticity of the real bills doctrine, while at the same time maintaining that the doctrine itself was not valid. The *Report* argues that as long as credit is restricted to "productive" uses, there is little danger of overexpansion. There is a difference between this policy and the real bills doctrine. The real bills doctrine certainly states that credit for productive uses will not produce overexpansion, but in addition, it holds that real bills *always* represent a productive use of credit. The inflation of 1919–1920 proved the folly of this latter notion, and the board had discarded it. However, the board did retain the notion of "productive" credit as non-expansionary.

The reason the board assumed this position is clear; the real bills doctrine professes very well the ideology of bankers. If their functions are automatic, they cannot be blamed for inflations or deflations. The board presented this argument in terms that seemed to make a great deal of sense. "The volume

27. *Tenth Annual Report*, p. 34.

of credit will seldom be at variance with the volume of credit needs as they are reflected in the demands of productive industry as long as (1) the volume of trade, production, and employment, and (2) the volume of consumption are in equilibrium." [28] This is a very difficult statement with which to argue, but it is not a satisfactory guideline for policy makers. Whether or not the economy reaches equilibrium depends in part on the relationship between the rate of profit and the rate of interest. Balance between the two is not always easy to achieve. The board retained some parts of the real bills doctrine and discarded others. The remainder was merely a truism which might be extremely difficult to implement.

Though the board could simply maintain that productive credit was self-regulating, the reserve banks could not. Their job was to implement the system's day-to-day policy, and the board's specious guideline was not enough. The reserve banks needed a more practical, operative approach to credit regulation. Their proximity to the credit market, which required them to have a workable theory, also gave them the experience out of which such a theory might come. Bank officials, especially those in the New York Bank, were much more knowledgeable than the board about the operation of the credit system and were able to develop a clearer and simpler approach to policy, which could also be implemented.

During this period Strong and other reserve bank officials cast off the bonds of the real bills doctrine completely. In a memorandum to Strong in 1922, Carl Snyder, an economist with the New York Bank, wrote, "Does not this open up the question as to whether our idea of an 'elastic currency which will respond to the demands of business' is fundamentally unsound? Is it not probable that the so-called 'demands of business' are to all extents unlimited; and that the only restraint

28. Ibid.

which we can have upon rising prices is a limited currency and a limited amount of credit?"[29]

Later that year Strong showed that he agreed with this view. In a talk given to the Graduate Economics Club at Harvard on November 28, 1922, Strong gave what must rank as one of the most brilliant discussions ever of the functioning of the Federal Reserve System.[30] Speaking of the qualitative aspects of the Federal Reserve Act, Strong said:

Now as to the limitations which the Federal Reserve Act seeks to impose as to the character of paper which a reserve bank may discount. When a member bank's reserve balance is impaired, it borrows to make it good, and it is quite impossible to determine to what particular purpose the money so borrowed may have been applied. It is simply the net reserve deficiency caused by a great mass of transactions. The borrowing member bank selects the paper which it brings to the Reserve Bank for discount . . . with regard to various elements of convenience . . . and it makes little difference to the borrowing bank what transactions may have caused the impairment of its reserve, because the paper which it discounts with the Reserve Bank may have no relation whatever to the impairment which has arisen. To specify more exactly—because this is an important point—suppose a member bank's reserve became impaired solely because on a given day it had made a number of loans on the stock exchange; it might then come to us with commercial paper which it had discounted two months before and which had no relation whatever to the transactions of the day; and with the proceeds of the discount make good the impairment. If it was the design of the authors of the Federal Reserve Act to pre-

29. Carl Snyder memorandum to Benjamin Strong, March 1, 1922, p. 9. This memorandum is in the Benjamin Strong Collection of the Library of the Federal Reserve Bank of New York.

30. A copy of this paper is contained in the Strong Collection at the Federal Reserve Bank of New York. Lester Chandler has quoted extensively from this talk in his book *Benjamin Strong*; see pages 195–198. The entire paper is reprinted in W. Randolph Burgess, ed., *Interpretations of Federal Reserve Policy in the Speeches and Writings of Benjamin Strong* (New York: Harper, 1930).

vent these funds so advanced by Federal Reserve Banks from being loaned on the Stock exchange or to non-member state banks or in any other type of ineligible loan, there would be only one way to prevent the funds from being so used, and that is by preventing the member banks from making any ineligible loans whatsoever, or deny it loans if it had.

Strong showed that qualitative restrictions were no restrictions at all. He noted that the amount of paper discounted with the reserve banks was only 14 percent of their total loans and discounts. The member banks "undoubtedly had a very much larger amount of eligible paper than indicated by this small percentage, but, beyond that, a great mass of ineligible loans, and surely it cannot be claimed that the provisions of the Act, which specify so exactly what paper is eligible, can possibly have exercised any influence upon the applications of the proceeds of these loans by the member banks." While Strong no doubt agreed with the views later expressed in the *Tenth Annual Report*, he could see no means by which the system could act directly to implement them.

The situation pictured by Strong was the result of two features of American banking: first, as Strong noted, borrowing at the reserve banks is strictly *ex post facto* and was intended to be that way; and second, with fractional reserve banking a bank never needs to discount all or even a large portion of its assets to replenish its reserves. As long as a member bank's investments in eligible securities are large enough to make up any reserve deficiency, either one of these two facts is sufficient to render the real bills doctrine worthless as qualitative credit control. The Federal Reserve System was not granted qualitative control over the total investments of its member banks, only that small portion which might be presented for discount. Strong, Snyder, and others saw this fact and realized the need to use active policy tools to achieve their goals.

The Influence of the Real Bills
Doctrine on Federal Reserve Policy

Despite the evidence given above, Federal Reserve policy during the period from 1915 to 1923 is often pictured as having been dominated by the real bills doctrine. Even Benjamin Strong, whose clear understanding of Federal Reserve credit indicates that he at least was free from the taint of real bills, has been so accused.[31] The evidence clearly refutes the claim that system policy was based on the real bills doctrine. Why, then, does this mistaken notion still persist?

The answer seems to lie primarily with the conception of the Federal Reserve System's purpose found in the statements of policy makers during the early years. Basically, they believed that the Federal Reserve was created to accommodate the growth and development of trade, industry, and agriculture; this is the reason why so many of the pronouncements of system officials suggest belief in the real bills doctrine. Board members and reserve bank officials concentrated on the accommodation of business and the suppression of speculation, because that was clearly their mandate under the act. Their public duty was to make certain that American productive activities had a stable financial framework in which to develop. The purpose of the Federal Reserve System was not to maintain a stable price level, except where stable prices promoted growth, or to keep unemployment below a certain percentage of the labor force, or to keep interest rates low, except where business conditions warranted low rates. These goals were sought only to the extent that they complemented the accommodation of business; the principal function of the system was

31. See *Federal Reserve Structure and the Development of Monetary Policy*, p. 7. This work maintains that the whole system was committed to the real bills theory.

to avoid the sort of banking crises which had occurred periodically during the previous fifty years.

Most people, including many Federal Reserve officials, believed that providing credit to productive enterprises while withholding credit from speculative ventures would accomplish the desired results. Probably this policy would have worked, but unfortunately the Federal Reserve, given its available tools, could not do this directly. The Federal Reserve System was capable of affecting aggregate credit only. The system had no tools with which it could directly control separate aspects of this aggregate amount.

After 1923 the Federal Reserve continued to concentrate on providing ample funds to productive endeavors while restricting the use of credit for speculation. This policy did not stem from a strong commitment to the real bills doctrine, but rather from a valid interpretation of the Federal Reserve Act's original purpose. The goal remained the same even if the theory, and therefore the policy, used to secure results were changed. There are many indirect indications and at least one significant operational indication of this change.

The operational indication of the system's liberation from the real bills doctrine is reflected in its open market operations. While the Federal Reserve Act provided for open market operations by the Federal Reserve Banks, it is clear that these operations were never intended to become a principal method of control. Two facts make this clear. First, the interpretation of the act by those closest to its origin supports the contention that its primary purpose was to provide a passive discounting organization, or perhaps merely an emergency institution. Therefore, control was to be exerted through changes in the rate at which eligible securities were discounted by the reserve banks. Second, open market operations were intended primarily as a means by which the reserve banks could obtain an income during times when discounts were not sufficient.[32] The use of open market operations to make discount rates effective was foreseen, but the power of this action was not appreciated.

Open market operations, except in government securities, would have been principally a one-way process, because it was considered poor form to resell commercial bills or bankers' acceptances. While firms or banks might peddle their own bills on the open market, they did not particularly care to see them resold by others. In England this feeling was so strong that the Bank of England never resold the bills it had discounted. The bank used other methods to tighten the market. The reluctance to engage in the resale of commercial paper was indirectly acknowledged by Paul Warburg when he made the suggestion that the 2 percent bonds used as national bank note collateral be redeemed and reissued—one half as 3 percent, twenty-year bonds, and one half as one-year Treasury notes. He noted that the latter securities would be ideal for the credit operations of the Federal Reserve Banks.[33] The reissue was accomplished by the Federal Reserve Act. The debt flotation of World War I increased the system's potential sphere of action in open market operations. In Chart 9.3 the two main components of open market purchases from 1921 to 1923 are graphed: open market paper (primarily acceptances), and government securities. Though the trend line of the two com-

32. Glass and particularly Willis maintained that this was one of the shortcomings of the Aldrich Bill: that it did not allow open market operations. This was a touchy subject because open market purchases or sales by the reserve banks would place them in direct competition with their member banks. See Willis, *The Federal Reserve System*, p. 331.

33. See Paul M. Warburg, "The Owen-Glass Bill," in *Essays on Banking Reform by Paul M. Warburg*, and also Willis, *The Federal Reserve System*, pp. 185–186, where a memorandum on the provisions of the proposed bill is attributed to Warburg.

ponents is virtually the same, it is clear that government securities were the agency used by the system to affect credit. The level of acceptances purchased is almost constant, while government securities show wide variation. The change in credit granted in the open market did not come from changes in the system's purchases of real bills.

Moral suasion, once known as direct action, was also an admission by the Federal Reserve Board that the character of the system's loans and discounts could not ensure that the act's commercial purpose would be carried out. Many other policy proposals indicate the unwillingness of the system to commit its policy to the real bills doctrine. It is certainly true that system officials believed their duty was to aid commerce. However, if the system's policy makers believed in the real bills doctrine as strongly as some claim, they would not and could not have acted as they did.[34]

34. For a similar conclusion about the lack of belief in the real bills doctrine on the part of system officials see Wicker, *Federal Reserve Policy*, pp. 63–66.

CHAPTER 10

The Structure of the Federal Reserve

Compromises and changes in the structure of the Federal
Reserve System were required if the goals of the system were
to be attained. The Federal Reserve System's organizational
features were shaped by its dependence on the real bills doctrine, and it is not surprising that organizational stresses appeared during the system's early years. Although these stresses
are well known, and much has been written about them either
directly or in relation to other aspects of Federal Reserve history,[1] few studies view the organizational stresses which developed during the period between 1914 and 1923 as being
connected with the theoretical foundation of the act. More
often they are seen as the result of imperfections in the structure of the system. Another common view is that the stresses
resulted from attempts to subvert the true purpose of the Federal Reserve Act; the chief culprits are generally either the
Treasury or the New York Bank. While all these opinions
contain an element of truth, in the main the stresses resulted

1. See, for instance, Chandler, *Benjamin Strong;* A. Jerome Clifford,
The Independence of the Federal Reserve System (Philadelphia: Uni-
versity of Pennsylvania Press, 1965); W. P. G. Harding, *The Formative
Period of the Federal Reserve System* (Boston and New York: Hough-
ton Mifflin, 1925); Seymour E. Harris, *Twenty Years of Federal Re-
serve Policy* (Cambridge, Mass.: Harvard University Press, 1933); and
William O. Weyforth, *The Federal Reserve Board* (Baltimore: The
Johns Hopkins Press, 1933.)

because the act placed excessive reliance on the real bills doctrine.[2] This excessive reliance made Willis, Glass, and others more willing to compromise on questions of control and organization. Their belief that the real bills doctrine would more or less automatically control the system made questions of control and organization less important. It is clear that from the beginning Glass and Willis gravitated toward provisions instituting extremely weak relations between the parts of the system.[3]

The Real Bills Doctrine and the Structure of the Federal Reserve System

The effects of the real bills doctrine on the structure of the Federal Reserve System resulted from the supposed automaticity of the discount activities of the reserve banks. While Willis, and perhaps also Glass, did not intend the system to operate only during emergencies, their view of its operations did not include overt control of money and credit. Rather, they saw the function of the Federal Reserve as aiding the development of the business sector by providing a market for commercial securities and a source of liquid capital for commercial enterprises. If the system's activities were in fact effectively limited by the real bills theory, only the loosest form of organization was necessary. This partially explains the almost complete decentralization which was the primary characteristic of the earliest versions of the Glass Bill.

2. At least one work attempts to relate the real bills doctrine to the structure and performance of the system, the House report, *Federal Reserve Structure and the Development of Federal Reserve Policy: 1915–1935*. This report is incorrect on two counts. First, the report demonstrates a lack of knowledge about the Federal Reserve Act as it was seen by those who drafted it, particularly with regard to its structure. Second, the report is incorrect in its statements about the extent of the effects of the real bills doctrine on the operation of the Federal Reserve System from 1914 to 1923.

3. See Chapters 5 and 6.

Given their beliefs, Glass and Willis could argue that since the reserve banks were confined primarily to operations in real bills offered by members for rediscount, there simply was no need for centralization. The local reserve banks were best able to determine the worthiness of paper offered to them. These regional banks would also be most familiar with the credit needs of their own regions. The result was a plan with an unspecified number of reserve banks (the first Glass Bill had "no less than fifteen")[4] with only a very loose form of organization. The real bills doctrine made an easy alliance with the political necessity of decentralization, which was a prime political consideration for the Democratic majority. The Democratic party was ideologically committed to reform; but in the case of banking, the commitment also included decentralization. This commitment appears in the Subtreasury system, the Fowler Bill, and many other Democratic proposals. There is little direct evidence that congressmen were aware of this relationship.

Only two arguments really existed against the degree of decentralization originally desired by Glass and Willis. First, there was the contention that a very large number of banks would not adequately marshal the country's reserves for use during financial emergencies. There was also a corollary to this argument: a large number of small banks would not be individually as strong as a small number of large banks. These contentions caused a decrease in the number of banks proposed, and a provision allowing the board to require interbank rediscounts.

The second argument against decentralization was that some central direction was necessary for the system to function properly. Since this idea implied control of the monetary and

4. Willis, *The Federal Reserve System*, p. 1532. See also Chapter 5 of this work.

credit system, the plan was not well received at the time. As a result, the argument for central control was made carefully in order not to arouse the enemies of the Money Trust. The situation was curious. The authors of the act seem to have believed that its operation would be relatively automatic with little need for centralized decision-making. Reformers who felt differently, who believed that coordination of monetary and credit policy was necessary, were not in a position to influence the legislation. Their intentions were suspect because of the wide public and congressional fear of the Money Trust and dominance by Wall Street. Ironically, bankers, especially New York bankers, were the people who best understood the workings and the needs of the financial sector. The question was whether or not the actions of this rather closely knit group were in the public interest. Certainly the Wall Street group desired more centralization and control than the Congress. It is likely that Wall Street men such as Warburg, Vanderlip, and Davison viewed themselves as acting in the public interest, even if others did not. At any rate, the widespread fear of the Money Trust and a degree of personal animosity caused Willis and Glass to disregard the views of many experienced and knowledgeable bankers.

By stressing automaticity, the real bills doctrine made structural questions less important and allowed their settlement in a manner consistent with the prevailing political climate, which demanded that the system at least appear to be relatively decentralized. In view of the powers granted to the board, one cannot say that the system was decentralized, but it had the semblance of decentralization which was important at the time.

Questions of Structure and Control, 1914–1923

Once the debate had ended and the Federal Reserve Act was law, the system faced the task of organizing for action. The first step was the determination of the location and number of Federal Reserve Banks. Also among the first orders of business was the selection of the Federal Reserve Board. Later came the selection of the officers of the reserve banks. After this initial period of organization, the banks actually opened approximately eleven months after the signing of the act.

Hardly had these problems been solved and the system been put into operation than a host of more difficult problems were faced. Prime among these was the location of final authority. There were three contestants for this prize: the Treasury, the banks, and the board. The struggle continued beyond our period, and a legislative settlement was not begun until 1935. A partial settlement came with the Treasury-Federal Reserve Accord in 1951. The lack of a clear-cut predominance by any one of the three groups from 1914 until 1923, and the resulting power struggle, explains much of the system's history during the first ten years.

Initial Organization of the Federal Reserve

Under the Federal Reserve Act, the secretary of the treasury, the secretary of agriculture, and the comptroller of the currency were to comprise the organization committee. Because these men were all political appointees, the wisdom of this provision was suspect. As it turned out, the organization committee was probably not free from political influence in its decisions. In addition to this committee, a separate group, headed by H. Parker Willis, was chosen to attend to the internal organization of the banks. This latter group was concerned with procedural matters such as accounting and record keeping.

Chief among the matters faced by the organization committee were the number and location of the reserve banks. The districting of the country was a minor concern, since it would follow rather naturally from the choice of the locations of reserve banks, but there had been an intense struggle over the number of banks. Glass and Willis had supported a provision requiring more than fifteen, perhaps one for every reserve city under the National Banking Act. The Senate and most bankers desired fewer banks. The Federal Reserve Act finally gave the organization committee some latitude in the matter. The committee could choose to establish as few as eight banks, or as many as twelve. There was a strong argument in favor of the creation of ten banks, but Secretary of the Treasury McAdoo and Comptroller of the Currency John Skelton Williams early decided to establish the full number.[5] This choice tended to make reserve banks outside the major financial centers very weak relative to the Boston, New York, and Philadelphia banks.

There were some obvious choices for the placement of reserve banks. New York, Boston, Philadelphia, Chicago, and San Francisco were major financial centers in their regions and in the nation as well. St. Louis was still a central reserve city under the National Banking System and deserved consideration because of its position in trade and the quality of its banking community, but St. Louis recently had been losing some of its business to New Orleans. Since New Orleans was also a prime candidate, there was a conflict. Another important financial center which received consideration was Baltimore.

Given the population distribution and also the distribution of manufacturing and trade—three factors which were obviously related—it was clear that the eastern districts would be smaller than those in the West. The necessity of encompassing adequate banking capital to form reserve banks west of the Mississippi would, by itself, ensure that the western districts would be larger. Therefore, the geographical size of the districts

5. See Willis, *The Federal Reserve System*, pp. 583–585.

was never a major concern of the organization committee. The committee attempted to consider the natural flow of business in addition to the distribution of population, trade, and manufacturing. With all these considerations, it was clear that some committee choices would be necessarily artificial.

The organization committee finally selected twelve cities: Boston, New York, Philadelphia, Richmond, Atlanta, Cleveland, Chicago, Minneapolis, St. Louis, Kansas City, Dallas, and San Francisco. The questionable nature of some choices is evident; Baltimore and New Orleans, for instance, were much more reasonable choices than Richmond, Atlanta, and Dallas. Pittsburgh perhaps would have been a better choice than Cleveland for the Mideast. Kansas City and Minneapolis could easily have been absorbed into the districts of St. Louis and Chicago, respectively. Then, the total number would have been nine, allowing three more banks to be established in the future, probably one in the South and two in the West, as the nation's growth might warrant.

Some choices had decidedly political overtones: Richmond was located in the state represented by Carter Glass; Colonel E. M. House, the president's closest personal confidant, was from Texas. Both of these men were in a position to influence the deliberations of the organization committee.

The result was a system of twelve reserve banks, some of which obviously were unable to stand on their own. Indeed, some banks had difficulty meeting the act's capital requirements. The minimum capital for a reserve bank was $4 million. The estimated capital of the four largest reserve banks created by the organization committee varied from $20,687,606, $12,967,701, $12,500,738 to $12,100,384, for New York, Chicago, Philadelphia, and Cleveland, respectively, but Atlanta and Minneapolis, the two smallest banks, had only $4,702,925 and $4,702,558. Richmond cleared the minimum only because its district included Baltimore and Washington, D.C. Two other reserve banks, in Dallas and Kansas City, had an estimated capital of less than $6 million each, and the St. Louis Bank only slightly exceeded the $6 million figure. This wide disparity did not deter the committee from creating the full number of reserve banks.

Many of the problems with the organization committee's selections were as clear then as they are now. A movement began almost immediately to reduce the number of reserve banks and was supported by a majority of the Federal Reserve Board. The secretary of the treasury was able to head off this change in structure only by eliciting from the attorney general an opinion that this action would go beyond the board's powers.

From the beginning it was clear that some reserve banks were destined to dominate the rest; in particular, those banks with more than adequate capital, located in cities where established money and credit markets existed. Among them, power naturally gravitated toward New York, where the nation's major money market was located and where banking expertise was the greatest. The organization committee would have found it difficult to organize a system giving more power to New York, than to create the maximum number of banks and to ensure that some of them would be dependent on the others.[6] Not only would a smaller number of banks have made New York less dominant, but such a large number made it probable that only one reserve bank, New York, would be capable of extending aid to other banks which were in trouble, should that occur.

All the predictions made by opponents of a large number of

6. This was the real, professed fear of Glass, Willis, and others—that New York, i.e., Wall Street, would control the system. Warburg warned at the Subcommittee Hearings that by holding out for a large number of reserve banks they would accomplish exactly what they wished to avoid. See Hearings, p. 64.

banks rapidly came true. Besides the dominance of New York, other problems soon developed. Some reserve banks, especially those in New York, Boston, and Philadelphia, had most of their money invested in rapidly maturing commercial loans of the "ideal" type. Other banks quickly became burdened under the sort of long-term agricultural loan which was the illegitimate son of the real bills family. Three banks, Minneapolis, Kansas City, and Dallas, consistently held more than 50 percent of the system's agricultural paper with a maturity of more than ninety days.[7] As a result, some reserve banks were less able to respond to credit demands which were ideally the concern of the system as a whole. New York, for instance, carried the brunt of federal financing during the war.[8] This strengthened the position of the New York Bank vis-à-vis the rest of the banks and also with regard to the Treasury and the board.

The Locus of Power

The location of ultimate power within the Federal Reserve was one of the most serious problems faced by the new system. Two factors—the real bills doctrine and the commitment to decentralization—determined the structure of the Federal Reserve System. The act had created a series of seemingly independent reserve banks and a coordinating agency called the Federal Reserve Board. All of these entities had clearly defined powers and spheres of action, or so it seemed. Both Willis and Glass at first desired that the power of action be concentrated in the reserve banks. Had not Wilson insisted on having a board, Willis and Glass would probably have resisted its creation. The lukewarm support they provided for the concept

7. See *The Annual Report of the Federal Reserve Board* for the years 1915–1923.
8. See *The Fifth Annual Report of the Federal Reserve Board* (Washington, D.C.: GPO, 1919), p. 168.

caused the act to be vague about the location of ultimate responsibility. Provisions necessary for coordination, such as the section concerning interbank rediscounting, were really only concessions to strong criticism of the independent reserve bank concept, and were not the expression of a desire to give final authority over policy to the board. The result left the locus of power ill defined.

The matter could have been resolved in four ways. First of all, as Willis and Glass had probably intended, each reserve bank could have gone its separate way except in times of emergency when policy would have been coordinated by the board. Because of the weakness of certain banks, this course was never a real possibility. A second outcome could have been for the reserve banks themselves to act in concert to control policy. This outcome would have made the board a useless appendage. Third, there was the possibility of the Federal Reserve Board directly controlling the system, and a fourth possible solution was Treasury control. There was justification for all of these possibilities either in the direct wording of the act or in the sense of the act. The rationale for the first two possibilities needs no elaboration. The third possibility—direct control by the board—comes not so much from a literal interpretation of the act, but from the view that the board was imbued with a public purpose, which was clearly Wilson's position. The board's right to power was based on the argument that the reserve banks primarily represented the member banks, and thus, the board by virtue of its public nature was the logical place for power to reside. The premise was that the public interest and the interest of the member banks might not always coincide. If there was a conflict, the people's representatives, the Federal Reserve Board, should be the ultimate authority.

As for the Treasury, its claim to power lay in a cryptic passage from section ten of the Federal Reserve Act, which reads as follows:

Nothing in this Act contained shall be construed as taking away any powers heretofore vested by law in the Secretary of the Treasury which relate to the supervision, management, and control of the Treasury Department and bureaus under such department, and wherever any power vested by this Act in the Federal Reserve Board or the Federal reserve agent appears to conflict with the powers of the Secretary of the Treasury, such powers shall be exercised subject to the supervision and control of the Secretary.

Broadly interpreted, this pasage could put vast powers in the hands of the secretary of the treasury.

From 1914 until 1923, three groups competed for power; each group had periods of ascendency and decline, and no clear-cut locus of power emerged. Action was often delayed and many questionable decisions were reached because of this competition.

Virtually all of the organizational problems during the early years came from two sources. The first was the early determination that the system's proper role was not the passive sort implied by a literal reading of the Federal Reserve Act. The second was the realization that as a guide to policy the real bills doctrine was inadequate, but this notion could not affect developments until after the war. However, the concept of positive central banking created stress from the very beginning. These two factors interacted to force the realization that coordinated, really centralized, action was necessary.

The first attempt to create an extralegal body to develop such coordination occurred shortly after the formation of the reserve banks. It was called the Conference of Governors and consisted of all twelve governors of the reserve banks. Willis, then secretary of the Federal Reserve Board, held that the origin of the Conference of Governors was obscure.[9] Its purpose was clear, however; it was formed to coordinate the policies of the twelve banks. The concentration of money markets in only a

9. Willis, *The Federal Reserve System*, p. 703.

few cities, principally in New York, necessitated some coordination of investment operations. The problem of the New York Bank was particularly delicate because its actions in the money market might be offset by the actions of other reserve banks. For instance, if the New York Bank felt that New York money rates were too low, it might move to raise them, but if some other bank was buying in the New York securities market, there might be no net result. Coordination of the activities of the banks would prevent this kind of conflict. In addition, officials such as Benjamin Strong, who had a larger conception of the system's purpose, were able to acquire the backing of all the reserve banks for purchases or sales if these activities were allocated among the banks.

Some people saw the Conference of Governors as an attempt to create the central bank which the Democrats had rejected.[10] The board viewed it as a usurpation of its own legally granted powers. As a result, W. P. G. Harding, second governor of the board, moved to restrict the freedom of action of the conference, because the board saw itself as the representative of the public interest. Governor Harding held the view that while the conference was no doubt useful, it should meet only when called by the Federal Reserve Board.[11] This conflict was left unresolved when World War I intervened; all such questions were submerged by the war effort.

During the war years the Treasury dominated money matters. Nearly all domestic considerations were subordinated to the war effort; the overriding concern was how to finance the war. Financial operations were in the hands of the Treasury, and Federal Reserve policy was coordinated to government debt offerings. The entire system willingly participated in this

10. This is the view given by Willis in The Federal Reserve System, p. 711, in sharp contrast to Chandler, Benjamin Strong, pp. 69–70.
11. See Chandler, Benjamin Strong, pp. 73–74.

change of focus. A sense of public duty—if not patriotism—was the main source of Federal Reserve support for Treasury policies. There was apparently never any need to resort to coercion, although the existence of the Overman Act was threat enough to all governmental agencies.

Because the Federal Reserve Board had no direct power over actual monetary and financial operations, the Treasury found it increasingly convenient to deal directly with the New York Bank. This was sometimes true regarding the Treasury and other banks as well. The net organizational result of the war was to increase the relative power of the reserve banks at the expense of the power of the board.[12] In large part this was due to the New York bank's position astride the nation's principal money market. As governor of the New York Bank, Benjamin Strong also had much to do with the institution's preeminence. He was the most knowledgeable and experienced of system officials. When Paul Warburg's term expired in 1917 and he was not reappointed, the board lost the one man who had both the stature in the business community and the practical knowledge which would have enabled the board to retain its prestige. The reasons Warburg was not reappointed should be obvious; but it is equally obvious that if he had remained on the board, the relationship between the New York Bank, the board, and the Treasury would have been subject to much less stress. Strong and Warburg were close friends, products of the same professional background. Their correspondence during the early years shows that their views about money and credit policy were very similar, even if they did not always agree. The presence of both these men in the councils of the Federal Reserve would have encouraged more coordinated policy. During the war and for a short time afterward, the board was not an active participant in policy making but rather the means by

12. See ibid., pp. 107, 115.

which the Treasury attempted to carry out its views when it could not reach agreement with the banks. There was substantial agreement on policy between the board and the Treasury, so the idea that the Treasury was dominant is only partly true; it was to become even less true as time passed.

When the war ended, the struggle for power appeared to be between the banks and the Treasury, with the board caught in the middle. But the situation was actually much more complex. What began as a struggle between the banks and the Treasury, after a time also became a struggle between the banks and the board. Again, it was a question of who represented the "public interest." The Treasury felt that the public interest demanded that the system create conditions favorable to the servicing of government debt. There was no small amount of covert pressure on the board to go along with the Treasury's desires, but the board was in substantial agreement with the Treasury, anyway. At the same time, the banks also felt that they were operating in the public interest. The issue was whether the threat to debt servicing offered by the proposed higher rates outweighed the potential economic consequences of an excessively easy money policy.

Any asessment of this debate involves at least a partial value judgment, but it is clear that the Treasury's main concern was the government's interest, rather than the public interest. Since the government had not been willing to raise revenue by increasing taxes, too much war financing had depended on debt issues. The Treasury was now faced with the results of this choice. In the end, the Federal Reserve found itself blamed, at least in part, for the effects of the policy choice made by the government during the war. Had the system been independent and free from these quasi-political forces, it might have responded quite differently to existing economic conditions. From the end of the war until the end of 1919, after the political danger of agression was ended, the system continued to function just like a government bank. The board's control over changes in the discount rate allowed the Treasury to negate any attempt by the banks to tighten credit.[13]

After 1919 it rapidly became clear that the real struggle was between the board and the banks. Between 1919 and 1935, when the board legally gained ascendency over the rest of the system, the power of the board increased. That is, its power increased in the sense that if agreement with the banks could not be reached, the board was more and more able to make its own views prevail. Forceful personalities outside the board, particularly Benjamin Strong, were able to influence system policy as much—and sometimes, more—than individual board members. Nevertheless, the tendency was for an increasing shift of power to the board.

Policy and Control

These organizational stresses and the resulting contests over supremacy in the system are illustrated most sharply in the struggles over control of the two major policy tools: changes in the rate of discount, and open market operations. The location of the control over these obviously crucial policy elements was an issue which was continually contested from 1914 until 1923. Because the use of open market operations as a policy tool did not develop until after the war, for the first five years or so, the struggle over the power to set the rate of discount was in effect a struggle for policy control.

Section fourteen of the Federal Reserve Act states that every Federal Reserve Bank shall have power "to establish from time to time, subject to review and determination of the Federal Reserve Board, rates of discount to be charged by the Federal

13. For a discussion of the results of this action on economic conditions and system policy, see Chapter 9.

reserve bank for each class of paper, which shall be fixed with a view of acommodating commerce and business."

The interpretation placed on this passage depended on two factors: first, belief about the intent of the law; and second, one's location in the organizational structure of the system.

It is important that the role of the discount rate in contemporary economic thought be understood. The discount rate was considered to be a central bank's most reliable tool. In large part this belief was due to the Bank of England's apparent success in using bank rate to regulate not only the British economy, but also the international gold standard. The received view of the Bank of England's rate manipulations generally ignored the difficulty with which the bank maintained their efficacy.[14] As a result, interest theory as applied to the monetary sector was in a very simple state. We can recall that the Aldrich Bill required a uniform rate of discount over the entire country. This part of the bill came under severe criticism by Glass and Willis, and it is probable that Warburg also disagreed with it. The Federal Reserve Act provided that the discount rate might vary among the districts. The question was related to the reserve bank concept, part of which held that a regional bank would be most competent to judge the credit situation in its district.

Allowing reserve banks to charge differing discount rates did not solve one problem which the opponents of uniform rates feared. Specifically, it was argued that in less-developed districts where the natural rate of interest was higher than the discount rate, uniform rates might cause excessive credit expansion. The opposite was also feared: excessively high rates in developed areas might lead to a stifling of growth. Would the uniform rate be based on the credit situation in developed

14. See, for example, Sayers, *Bank of England Operations*. See also Chapter 8.

areas or underdeveloped areas? Under the rate structure of the Federal Reserve System, such problems were not eliminated. To use Willis's own example: "For instance, an Atlanta bank which desired to get a large line of rediscounts might arrange with a New York institution to rediscount for it with the Federal Reserve Bank of New York, such paper of course taking the New York rate which might be a little lower than the rate prevailing in Atlanta. This practice tended greatly to interfere with the development of the local discount market in the several districts which had been so earnestly desired."[15] It should have been obvious that funds would tend to flow from low interest areas to high interest areas regardless of the form of the interest provision or the structure of the system. Such a process is the way in which interest rate differentials are neutralized,[16] and it is similar to the process by which other factor prices tend to be equalized.

Again the regional concept had led to the adoption of a specific provision. Any discussion of the discount rate provision must begin by considering the objectives of the Federal Reserve Act. The clear intent of the act was that future development was to be consistent with the act's most important feature—its regional structure. The reserve banks were given powers which it was hoped would be sufficient to allow them to develop independently, especially regarding local credit markets. Willis's statement bears this out. This interpretation, if it is correct, conflicts with the Federal Reserve Board's claim to power over the discount rate.

15. Willis, *The Federal Reserve System*, p. 897.

16. Such a trend had been proceeding for some years. See two articles by Lance E. Davis: "Capital Immobilities and Finance Capitalism: A Study of Economic Evolution in the United States 1820–1920," *EEH*, ser. 2, 1 (Fall 1963), 88–105; and "The Investment Market, 1870–1914: The Evolution of a National Market," *Journal of Economic History*, 25 (Sept. 1965), 355–399.

Even Willis admitted that the board went beyond the intentions of the act when they took control over the rate of discount, although he probably felt it was both wise and necessary.
In his words: "Thus the Board practically took to itself a substantially larger power than had originally been granted by the
framers of the act. . . . The general question whether it was
or was not desirable for the Board to exercise the powers which
it thus in the circumstances usurped never came to an issue in
any overt way."[17]

This usurpation, to use Willis's description, occurred when
the Federal Reserve Board informed the reserve banks that
each week they would be required to submit their proposed
discount rates to the board for approval. Since the board had
the power to disapprove any proposed rate, a bank which was
out of line with the board's conception of the proper rate
would have to resubmit its rate proposals. This procedure
certainly went beyond both the intent and the wording of the
act. While Willis seems to have accepted the board's action as
the best course, Glass appeared on both sides of the issue. In
late 1919, after the banks had spent the better part of the year
attempting to raise rates, Glass, then secretary of the treasury,
and Strong had a sharp disagreement over the board's power
to control the discount rate. Glass asked the attorney general
for an opinion on the matter. The legal opinion supported the
board's contention. However, once Glass was back in the
Senate, his views changed. When, in 1927, the board ordered
the Federal Reserve Bank of Chicago to lower its rates, Glass
maintained that such action was clearly illegal.[18] This is one
more indication of the ambiguity of the act. As conditions
changed, there was continued flux in the relations between the
banks, the board, and the Treasury.

Willis was mistaken in supposing that no issue was raised

17. Willis, The Federal Reserve System, pp. 892, 893.
18. See Chandler, Benjamin Strong, pp. 161–162.

when the board took over the power to initiate rate changes. The governors of the reserve banks immediately objected to this attempt by the board to increase its power.[19] But a combination of events postponed the showdown between the banks and the board. First, Benjamin Strong became ill early in 1916 and was absent from New York for some time. Second, the war intervened shortly thereafter, and the whole system closed ranks to aid the war effort. The crisis came in 1919 when the reserve banks continually insisted that rates be raised to slow the rate of inflation, a policy which the Treasury opposed. The result was the ruling from the attorney general favoring the board. Ironically, the attorney general issued his opinion on December 9, 1919, and the very next day the Treasury consented to an increase in the rate of discount. The board retained its power over the discount rate, but in this case at least, the banks demonstrated that they still had the ability to affect policy.

The discount rate was only one tool used by the Federal Reserve to affect the availability of credit. Even during the period of 1914 to 1923, the use of the discount rate was being supplemented by open market operations. Today, operations on the open market have become the major tool of the Federal Reserve System. During the early years, however, open market operations were generally viewed as subordinate or, at best, complementary to discount rate policy.

Open market operations emerged in an embryonic form a few weeks after the opening of the banks. The banks wished to use their resources profitably so that they could meet their expenses without resorting to such expedients as assessments on member banks. In the beginning, purchases consisted primarily of bankers' acceptances and municipal warrants. Since several of the banks had no well-developed market for these securities in their own districts, the New York Bank was soon

19. See ibid., pp. 70–71.

engaging in open market operations for other banks, but the timing of sales and purchases was not coordinated. This lack of coordination soon began to have potentially disturbing effects on the money markets. As a result, Strong suggested in 1916 that purchases be coordinated through a committee of governors,[20] a proposal which was not adopted at the time. The issue lay dormant until 1921.

Late in 1921 the system began large purchases of government securities, again primarily for the purposes of augmenting their earning assets.[21] The purchases had a highly salutary effect on the economy which was still recovering from the depression of 1920–1921.[22] The continuance of these purchases during 1922 demonstrated their effects much more clearly and pointed out the need for coordinated operations. As a result, in 1922 the governors created "The Committee of Governors on Centralized Execution of Purchases and Sales of Government Securities by Federal Reserve Banks," commonly known as the Governors' Committee. This was not a policy committee but rather a committee charged with coordinating the execution of the orders placed by the individual reserve banks. The governors of the Boston, New York, Philadelphia, Cleveland, and Chicago Banks made up the Governors' Committee. Even though this committee was not a direct policy making body, it came to have increasing influence over policy matters.

Again, as in the case of the creation of the Conference of Governors before the war, this body rapidly came into conflict with the board. The conflict surfaced while Strong was away recuperating in Colorado. The board disbanded the Governors' Committee only to appoint the same men to a new committee

20. See ibid., pp. 76–78.

21. Chart 9.3 shows the extent of these purchases of government securities. It also compares purchases of government securities with purchases of acceptances.

22. Chandler argues that the New York Bank had other purposes in mind. See Chandler, *Benjamin Strong*, pp. 210–211.

called the "Open Market Investment Committee for the Federal Reserve System." This new committee was to operate under the supervision of the Federal Reserve Board, and according to its regulations. As far as structural matters go, creation of the Open Market Investment Committee signaled the advent of two closely related changes: first, the power of the reserve banks to affect policy was being substantially reduced; second, open market operations were to become completely centralized under the board's supervision.

It was not clear whether the board had the power to act as it did. The chief advocate of extending the board's power was Adolph Miller, a board member who was also a professional economist. Miller firmly believed that the board's power should be extended over the entire system, but Strong, along with other governors, disagreed strenuously. In the end, the board prevailed. The trend toward centralization of power in the board was not accompanied by the same kind of argument which had occurred in Congress over the act's structural provisions. It was now generally recognized that centralization of power was both necessary and wise, the disagreement was over the locus of that power.

Structural Change: An Assessment

A landmark Federal Reserve *Annual Report* was written in 1923. The *Report* gave a different character to the system's theoretical basis, and that same year marked the culmination of a trend which modified the structure of the system. This structural change occurred as the board wrested control of the system's two major policy tools from the banks—a virtual assurance of the board's continued supremacy in policy matters.

The result of the structural modification was a Federal Reserve System very unlike the one intended. Given the evidence, it should be clear that the proponents of the Federal Reserve Act intended the reformed banking system to be

relatively decentralized. The modification was at least partially
a result of ambiguities in the act itself, which allowed differing
interpretations of the proper location of ultimate power.

This interpretation of the structural flux of the early years is
not universally accepted. Here, the transfer of power from the
banks to the board has been viewed as an organic and logical
evolution, an evolution forced by the realities of the American
monetary and credit sector. A very different interpretation is
found in the House Report, *Federal Reserve Structure and the
Development of Monetary Policy, 1915–1935*. That work proceeds directly from the premise that the Federal Reserve Act
originally intended that ultimate power was to reside in the
board. The banks are pictured in that report as attempting to
usurp the legitimate locus of power within the system. Such a
view cannot be accepted as valid, because the evidence in support of the intention to decentralize is much too strong.

The view taken in this work of a second aspect of this development reflects more of a value judgment. The trend toward
centralization was probably desirable. Centralization was,
from the beginning, desirable from an economic standpoint,
although it may have been politically impossible. The structure of the Federal Reserve System came more and more to
resemble the structure of the National Reserve System proposed by the Aldrich Bill. It also came to operate more and
more as the National Reserve System had been expected to
operate.

These structural trends proceeded almost without challenge
from outside the system; they may also have proceeded largely
without notice outside the system. The Federal Reserve Act
created a banking system which was not completely suited to
the reality of existing conditions in the American economy. A
large part of the system's energy during the first ten years was
spent in an attempt to come to terms with existing conditions.

CHAPTER 11

Epilogue: The Reform
Movement in Retrospect

In 1923 the *Tenth Annual Report* appeared to indicate that the transformation of American banking was complete. The Federal Reserve System seemed to have realized and defined its responsibilities and developed the means by which they could be carried out. Certainly the structure of the financial sector had been transformed, and a new era had begun. It was believed that the financial panics and depressions that had plagued the nineteenth-century economy had been eliminated.

In spite of this optimism there was cause for concern. The experience of the previous sixty years still strongly influenced the views of many important policy makers. Their somewhat obsolete views of credit and the role of the banking system in the economy did not have harmful consequences as long as the economy was healthy. The emphasis on accommodation, a natural outgrowth of the reform movement, meant that the Federal Reserve System would do all in its power to sustain growth. As it turned out, this emphasis was an obstacle to effective action during economic downswings. The Federal Reserve Board's reaction to the financial crisis in 1933 makes little sense unless one considers the issue of accommodation. The board in its *Annual Report* congratulated itself for handling the crisis so well. Apparently the board felt that way because there had been no difficulty in converting deposits into currency. The fall in the stock of money and the decline in national income did not trouble the board; the former was merely an accommodation to the latter. During this period the Federal Reserve Bank of New York stood almost alone in calling for monetary expansion. The rest of the system was content to let the stock of money accommodate itself to the decline in business.

The different views within the system reflect the differing impacts of the experiences of the first decade. Banking reform was continuing even though no new major laws were being passed. In this study banking reform has meant more than the mere advancement of proposals and their acceptance or rejection. It includes the change in ideas and the debate over the structure and theory of laws about to be passed, or which had already been passed. This is why the years from 1914 to 1923 have been considered a period of reform just as have the years from 1907 to 1913.

Two issues appear to have been extremely important to the development of banking reform in the United States: the acceptance of the real bills theory, and the question of organization. To a large degree what reformers felt about these two matters determined the course of banking development.

The influence of the real bills doctrine on the framers of the Federal Reserve Act, and thus on the act itself, has been shown. The real bills doctrine provided not only the theoretical foundation of the act's discounting provisions but also a complementary rationale for the bill's structural aspects. This effect, or at least the extent of it, has often been denied.[1] On

1. See two papers by Clark Warburton, "Monetary Control under the Federal Reserve Act," *Political Science Quarterly*, 61 (Dec. 1946), 505–534, and "Coordination of Monetary, Bank Supervisory, and Loan Agencies of the Federal Government," *Journal of Finance*, 5 (June

the basis of the evidence presented in this study, the influence of this theoretically questionable doctrine appears great indeed. On the other hand, it has been argued here that the effects of the real bills doctrine on Federal Reserve operations and the theoretical underpinnings of Federal Reserve policy from 1914 to 1923 have been overstated.[2] The evidence suggests that by 1923 this theory's influence on policy had declined to nothing in some parts of the system, and appeared to be critically weakened in others. If this view is correct—and the evidence suggests it is—a reinterpretation of some aspects of Federal Reserve action may be in order.

The question of organization has been an important one in American society for a very long time. There should be no surprise that the issue arose with regard to banking reform. The choice turned out to be not between decentralization and centralization, but rather a determination of how far centralization was to proceed. From a political standpoint, and presumably from a theoretical standpoint as well, the choice was made between a relatively centralized system—the National Reserve System—and a regionally centralized one—the Federal Reserve System. The latter won out primarily because of the vagaries of politics. As subsequent events demonstrated, the Federal Reserve Act was constructed in a way that allowed its provisions to be used to establish what amounted to a central bank, though this was certainly not the declared intent of those who had drafted the act.

Eventually, the banking reform acts passed during the 1930's wrote the centralized nature of the system into law.

1950), 148–169. Warburton's presentation of Willis's views and the relationship between the real bills doctrine and the Federal Reserve Act differ sharply from the conclusions of this work.

2. See House Report, *Federal Reserve Structure and the Development of Monetary Policy, 1915–1935,* for the view that system policy was dominated by the real bills doctrine.

The Federal Reserve Board was made the principal policy body of the system and the reserve banks were reduced to mere appendages. Even with these legal changes in the system, the question of final monetary authority remained unresolved. The Federal Reserve System still was forced to compete with the Treasury Department. This rivalry was settled only in 1951 with the Treasury-Federal Reserve Accord. Today the Federal Reserve is in fact a central bank with almost autonomous control over monetary policy. Real economic and political pressures have caused this deviation from the intentions of the reformers, and future changes in economics or politics could cause further evolution.

The theory and organization of banking reform have been the major topics of this book. However, it is clear that the arguments discussed here have an impact on other aspects of the Federal Reserve. The overall task has been to place the Federal Reserve in its proper historical setting. This setting and an understanding of it are important for any study of Federal Reserve policy or development before 1951. It is often easy to assert *what* should have been done, but understanding *why* things happened as they did is often more important.

Bibliography

PAPERS AND CORRESPONDENCE

Laughlin, J. Laurence. Papers and Correspondence. The Library of Congress.

Strong, Benjamin. Papers and Correspondence. The Research Library of the Federal Reserve Bank of New York.

Willis, H. Parker. Papers and Correspondence. The Columbia University Libraries.

Papers in the Research Library of the Board of Governors of the Federal Reserve System

Goldenweiser, E. A. "Significance of the Lending Functions of the Federal Reserve Banks." Paper read before the annual meeting of the American Statistical Association, December 30, 1935.

Hamlin, C. S. "The Federal Reserve Established and in Operation." Address delivered before the New York Chamber of Commerce, December 3, 1914.

Harding, W. P. G. "The Functions and Policies of the Federal Reserve Board." Address before the Chamber of Commerce of Cleveland, Ohio, September 16, 1920.

———. "The Present Position and the Future Development of the Federal Reserve System." Address before the Forum of the New York Chapter of the Institute of Banking, November 1, 1916.

Miller, Adolph C. "American Banking: Control of the Credit System," *London Times Annual Financial Review*, January 23, 1920. Copy in Library of the Board of Governors of the Federal Reserve System.

GOVERNMENT PUBLICATIONS

Andrew, A. Piatt. *Monetary Statistics for the U.S. 1867–1909.* Washington, D.C.: GPO, 1910.

Breckenridge, Roeliff Morton. *The History of Banking in Canada.* Washington, D.C.: GPO, 1910.

Cannon, James Graham. *Clearing Houses.* Washington, D.C.: GPO, 1910.

Davis, Andrew McFarland. *The Origin of the National Banking System.* Washington, D.C.: GPO, 1910.

——. *Supplement to the Origin of the National Banking System.* Washington, D.C.: GPO, 1911.

Dewey, Davis R. *State Banking before the Civil War.* Washington, D.C.: GPO, 1910.

Federal Reserve Board. *First [through Tenth] Annual Report of the Federal Reserve Board.* Washington, D.C.: GPO, 1915–1924.

Hollander, Jacob H. *Bank Loans and Stock Exchange Speculation.* Washington, D.C.: GPO, 1911.

Jacobs, Lawrence Merton. *Bank Acceptances.* Washington, D.C.: GPO, 1910.

Johnson, Joseph French. *The Canadian Banking System.* Washington, D.C.: GPO, 1910.

Kemmerer, E. W. *Seasonal Variations in the Relative Demand for Money and Capital in the United States.* Washington, D.C.: GPO, 1910.

Kinley, David. *The Independent Treasury of the U.S. and Its Relation to the Banks of the Country.* Washington, D.C.: GPO, 1910.

Noyes, Alexander Dana. *History of the National-Bank Currency.* Washington, D.C.: GPO, 1910.

United States Congress. *Congressional Record,* 63d Cong. Washington, D.C.: GPO, 1913.

——, House of Representatives. *Federal Reserve Structure and the Development of Monetary Policy: 1915–1935,* Staff Report of the Subcommittee on Domestic Finance, Committee on Banking and Currency, 92d Cong. Washington, D.C.: GPO, 1971.

——, House of Representatives. *Hearings before the Subcommittee on Banking and Currency Charged with Investigating Plans of Banking and Currency Reform,* 62d Cong. Washington, D.C.: GPO, 1913.

——, House of Representatives. *House Report 163,* 63d Cong. Washington, D.C.: GPO, 1913.

——, House of Representatives. *Report of Charles N. Fowler from the Committee on Banking and Currency, House Reports,* 60th Cong., Vol. 1, Report No. 1126. Washington, D.C.: GPO, 1908.

——, Senate. *Hearings on H.R. 7837 (S. 2639),* Senate Document 232, 63d Cong. Washington, D.C.: GPO, 1913.

——, Senate. *Senate Document 242,* 63d Cong. Washington, D.C.: GPO, 1913.

United States National Monetary Commission. *Interviews on the Banking and Currency Systems of Canada.* Washington, D.C.: GPO, 1910.

——. *Interviews on the Banking and Currency Systems of England, Scotland, France, Germany, Switzerland, and Italy.* Washington, D.C.: GPO, 1910.

——. *Laws of the U.S. Concerning Money, Banking, and Loans, 1778–1909.* Washington, D.C.: GPO, 1910.

——. *Letter from Secretary of the National Monetary Commission Transmitting Pursuant to Law, the Report of the Commission.* Washington, D.C.: GPO, 1912.

——. *Miscellaneous Articles on German Banking.* Washington, D.C.: GPO, 1910.

——. *The Reichsbank, 1876–1900.* Washington, D.C.: GPO, 1910.

United States Treasury Department. *Annual Report of the Comptroller of the Currency.* Washington, D.C.: GPO, 1889–1914.

——. *Annual Report on the State of the Finances.* Washington, D.C.: GPO, 1873. Secretary William A. Richardson.

Warburg, Paul M. *The Discount System in Europe.* Washington, D.C.: GPO, 1910.

BOOKS AND ARTICLES

American Bankers' Association. *Proceedings of the American Bankers' Association Convention, 1894.* New York: American Bankers' Association, 1894.

——. *Proceedings of the American Bankers' Association Convention, 1902.* New York: American Bankers' Association, 1902.

Anderson, Clay J. *A Half Century of Federal Reserve Policy Making, 1914–1964.* Philadelphia: The Federal Reserve Bank of Philadelphia, 1965.

Andrew, A. P. "Credit and the Value of Money," *Publications of the American Economic Association,* 6 (February 1905).

Ashton, T. S., and R. S. Sayers. *Papers in English Monetary History.* Oxford: Clarendon, 1953.

Barron, D. W. *The Federal Reserve Act.* Boston: Boston News Bureau, 1914.

Beckhart, Benjamin Haggot. *The Discount Policy of the Federal Reserve System.* New York: Holt, 1924.

——. *Federal Reserve System.* New York: American Institute of Banking, 1972.

Bloomfield, Arthur. *Monetary Policy under the Gold Standard, 1880–1914.* New York: Federal Reserve Bank of New York, 1959.

Burgess, W. Randolph, ed. *Interpretations of Federal Reserve Policy in the Speeches and Writings of Benjamin Strong.* New York: Harper, 1930.

——. *The Reserve Banks and the Money Market.* New York: Harper, 1936.

Chandler, Lester V. *Benjamin Strong, Central Banker.* Washington, D.C.: The Brookings Institution, 1958.

Clapham, Sir John. *The Bank of England,* 2 vols. Cambridge: The University Press, 1944.

Clark, Lawrence E. *Central Banking Under the Federal Reserve System.* New York: Macmillan, 1935.

Clifford, A. Jerome. *The Independence of the Federal Reserve System.* Philadelphia: University of Pennsylvania Press, 1965.

Coats, A. W., and William R. Allen. "The Interpretation of Mercantilist Economics: Some Historiographical Problems," *History of Political Economy,* 5 (Fall 1973).

Davis, Lance E. "Capital Immobilities and Finance Capitalism: A Study of Economic Evolution in the United States, 1820–1920," *EEH,* ser. 2, 1 (Fall 1963).

——. "The Investment Market, 1870–1914: The Evolution of a National Market," *Journal of Economic History,* 25 (September 1965).

Dewey, Davis Rich. *Financial History of the United States.* New York: Longmans, Green, 1931.

Diamond, William. *The Economic Thought of Woodrow Wilson.* Baltimore: The Johns Hopkins Press, 1943.

Fetter, Frank Whitson. *Development of English Monetary Orthodoxy.* Cambridge, Massachusetts: Harvard University Press, 1965.

Fisher, Irving. *The Theory of Interest.* New York: Macmillan, 1930.

Friedman, Milton, and Anna Jacobson Schwartz. *A Monetary History of the United States, 1867–1960.* Princeton: Princeton University Press, 1963.

Gallatin, Albert. *Suggestions on the Banks and Currency.* New York: Wiley and Putnam, 1841.

Glass, Carter. *An Adventure in Constructive Finance.* New York: Doubleday, 1927.

Goldenweiser, E. A. *Federal Reserve System in Operation.* New York: McGraw-Hill, 1925.

Goodhart, C. A. E. *The New York Money Market and the Finance of Trade, 1900–1913.* Cambridge: Harvard University Press, 1968.

Greef, Albert O. *The Commercial Paper House in the United States.* Cambridge: Harvard University Press, 1938.

Gregory, T. E. *Select Statutes, Documents and Reports Relating to British Banking, 1832–1928,* vol. II. Oxford: University Press, 1929.

Hammond, Bray. *Banks and Politics in America from the Revolution to the Civil War.* Princeton: Princeton University Press, 1957.

Harding, W. P. G. *The Formative Period of the Federal Reserve System.* Boston and New York: Houghton Mifflin, 1925.

Hardy, Charles O. *Credit Policies of the Federal Reserve System.* Washington, D.C.: The Brookings Institution, 1932.

Harris, S. E. *Twenty Years of Federal Reserve Policy.* 2 vols. Cambridge, Massachusetts: Harvard University Press, 1933.

Hawtrey, R. G. *The Gold Standard in Theory and Practice.* London: Longmans, Green, 1927.

Hepburn, A. B. *The Currency Problem and the Present Financial Situation.* New York: Columbia University Press, 1908.

——. *A History of Currency in the United States.* New York: Macmillan, 1924.

Hoyt, Edwin P. *The House of Morgan.* New York: Dodd, Mead, 1966.

Hughes, J. R. T. *Fluctuations in Trade, Industry and Finance.* Oxford: Clarendon, 1960.

——. "Wicksell on the Facts: Prices and Interest Rates, 1844–1914," in *Value, Capital and Growth: Papers in Honor of Sir John Hicks.* Edinburgh: Edinburgh University Press, 1968.

Kemmerer, Edwin Walter. *The ABC of the Federal Reserve System.* Princeton: Princeton University Press, 1932.

Kemmerer, Edwin W., and Donald L. Kemmerer. *The ABC of the Federal Reserve System.* New York: Harper, 1950.

Kemmerer, Edwin Walter. *Money and Credit Instruments in their Relation to General Prices.* New York: Holt, 1907.

King, W. T. C. *History of the London Discount Market.* London: Cass, 1972; reprint of 1936 edition.

Kinley, David. *Money.* New York: Macmillan, 1930; originally published 1904.

Klein, Joseph J. "Commercial Importance of Single Name Paper," *Annalist,* 3 (March 23, 1914).

Knox, John Jay. *A History of Banking in the United States.* New York: Kelly, 1969; originally published in 1903.

Kolko, Gabriel. *The Triumph of Conservatism.* Glencoe: The Free Press, 1963.

Kroos, Herman E., and Paul A. Samuelson. *Documentary History of Banking and Currency in the United States*, 4 vols. New York: Chelsea House and McGraw-Hill, 1969.

Lamont, Thomas W. *Henry P. Davison*. New York: Harper, 1933.

Laughlin, J. Laurence. "The Aldrich-Vreeland Act," *Journal of Political Economy*, 16 (October 1908).

——. "The Banking and Currency Act of 1913, I," *Journal of Political Economy*, 22 (April 1914).

——. *Banking Progress*. New York: Scribner's, 1920.

——, ed. *Banking Reform*. Chicago: Blakely, 1912.

——. *The Federal Reserve Act: Its Origin and Problems*. New York: Macmillan, 1933.

——. *Money Credit and Prices*. vol. II. Chicago: University of Chicago Press, 1931.

——. *The Principles of Money*. New York: Scribner's, 1926.

——. *Suggestions For Banking Reform*. Chicago: National Citizens' League, 1912.

——. "The Theory of Prices," *Papers and Proceedings of the American Economic Association*, 6 (February 1905).

Macaulay, Frederick Robertson. *The Movements of Interest Rates, Bond Yields and Stock Prices in the United States Since 1856*. New York: National Bureau of Economic Research, 1958.

Mints, Lloyd W. *A History of Banking Theory in Great Britain and the United States*. Chicago: University of Chicago Press, 1945.

Morawetz, Victor. "The Banking and Currency Problem and its Solution." *The Reform of the Currency, Proceedings of the Academy of Political Science*, 1 (January 1911).

——. *The Banking and Currency Problem in the United States*. New York: North American Review, 1909.

Morgenstern, Oskar. *International Financial Transactions and Business Cycles*. Princeton: Princeton University Press for NBER, 1959.

Muhleman, Maurice L. *Monetary and Banking Systems*. New York: Monetary Publishing Co., 1908.

——. "A Plan for a Central Bank," *Banking Law Journal*, 26 (November, December 1909); 27 (January, February, March 1910).

Mullins, Eustace Clarence. *A Study of the Federal Reserve*. New York: Casper and Horton, 1952.

Myers, Margaret G. *The New York Money Market*, vol. I. New York: Columbia University Press, 1931.

National Bank of Commerce. *Commercial Banking Practice Under the Federal Reserve Act*. New York: National Bank of Commerce, 1921.

Nishimura, Shizuya. *The Decline of Inland Bills of Exchange in the*

London Money Market 1855–1913. Cambridge: Cambridge University Press, 1971.

Owen, Robert L. *The Federal Reserve Act.* New York: Century, 1919.

Patterson, Raymond. *The Central Bank Controversy.* Boston: Chapple, 1910.

Phillips, Chester Arthur. *Bank Credit.* New York: Macmillan, 1921.

Prochnow, Herbert V., ed. *The Federal Reserve System.* New York: Harper, 1960.

Redlich, Fritz. *The Molding of American Banking,* 2 vols. New York: Hafner, 1947.

Reed, Harold L. *The Development of Federal Reserve Policy.* Boston: Houghton Mifflin, 1922.

——. *Federal Reserve Policy 1921–1930.* New York: McGraw-Hill, 1930.

Report of the Monetary Commission of the Indianapolis Convention of Boards of Trade, Chambers of Commerce, Commercial Clubs, and Other Similar Bodies of the United States. Indianapolis: Hollenbelk, 1900.

Riefler, Winfield W. *Money Rates and Money Markets in the United States.* New York and London: Harper, 1930.

Rist, Charles. *History of Monetary and Credit Theory from John Law to the Present Day.* London: Allen and Unwin, 1940.

Robertson, Dennis H. *A Study of Industrial Fluctuation.* London: King, 1915.

——. *Essays in Monetary Theory.* London: Staples, 1940.

Robinson, Roland I., et al. *Financial Institutions.* Homewood, Ill.: Irwin, 1960.

Satterlee, Herbert L. *J. Pierpont Morgan.* New York: Macmillan, 1939.

Sayers, R. S. *Bank of England Operations, 1890–1914.* London: P. S. King and Son, 1936.

——. *Central Banking after Bagehot.* Oxford: Clarendon, 1957.

Schultz, William J., and M. R. Caine. *Financial Development of the United States.* New York: Prentice-Hall, 1937.

Schumpeter, Joseph. *History of Economic Analysis.* New York: Oxford University Press, 1954.

Scott, William A. *Banking.* Chicago: A. C. McClurg, 1914.

——. *Money.* Chicago: McClurg, 1913.

——. *Money and Banking.* New York: Holt, 1926; originally published 1910.

Sherman, John. *Selected Speeches and Reports on Finance and Taxation.* New York: Appleton, 1879.

Smith, Adam. *An Inquiry into the Nature and Causes of the Wealth of Nations.* New York: Modern Library, 1937.

Smith, Vera C. *The Rationale of Central Banking.* London: P. S. King & Son, 1936.

Soule, George. *Prosperity Decade From War to Depression: 1917–1929.* New York: Holt, Rinehart and Winston, 1964.

Spahr, Walter Earl. *The Federal Reserve System and the Control of Credit.* New York: Macmillan, 1931.

Sprague, O. M. W. *History of Crises under the National Banking System.* New York: Kelly, 1968.

——. "The Organization of the Federal Reserve Banks," *Proceedings of the Academy of Political Science,* 4 (October 1913).

——. "The Proposal for a Central Bank in the United States: A Critical View," *Quarterly Journal of Economics,* 23 (May 1909).

Stephenson, Nathaniel Wright. *Nelson W. Aldrich.* New York: Scribner's, 1930.

Studenski, Paul and Herman E. Kroos. *Financial History of the United States.* New York: McGraw-Hill, 1963.

Sumner, William Graham. *A History of Banking in the United States.* New York: The Journal of Commerce and Commercial Bulletin, 1896.

Taus, Ester Rogoff. *Central Banking Functions of the U. S. Treasury, 1789–1941.* New York: Columbia University Press, 1943.

Temin, Peter. *The Jacksonian Economy.* New York: Norton, 1969.

Thornton, Henry. *An Inquiry into the Nature and Effects of the Paper Currency of Great Britain.* New York: Kelly, 1962.

Tooke, Thomas and William Newmarch. *A History of Prices,* with an introduction by T. E. Gregory. London: London School of Economics Reprints of Scarce Works on Political Economy, 1962.

Viner, Jacob. *Studies in the Theory of International Trade.* New York: Kelly, 1965.

Warburg, Paul M. "Central Bank of the United States," *Papers and Discussions of the Twenty-First Annual Meeting of the American Economic Association* (April 1909).

——. *The Federal Reserve System,* 2 vols. New York: Macmillan, 1930.

——. *Essays on Banking Reform by Paul M. Warburg, Proceedings of the Academy of Political Science,* 4 (January 1914).

Warburton, Clark. "Coordination of Monetary, Bank Supervisory, and Loan Agencies of the Federal Government," *Journal of Finance,* 5 (June 1950).

——. "Monetary Control under the Federal Reserve Act," in *Political Science Quarterly,* 61 (December 1946).

Weyforth, William O. *The Federal Reserve Board*. Baltimore: The Johns Hopkins Press, 1933.

White, Horace. "Assets Currency," *Proceedings of the American Bankers' Association Convention, 1902*. New York: The American Bankers' Association, 1902.

——. *Money and Banking*. Boston: Ginn, 1911; first edition in 1895.

Wicker, Elmus R. *Federal Reserve Monetary Policy 1917–1933*. New York: Random House, 1966.

Wicksell, Knut. "The Influence of the Rate of Interest on Prices," *Economic Journal*, 17 (June 1907).

Willis, Henry Parker. *The Federal Reserve*. Garden City: Doubleday, Page, 1915.

——. *The Federal Reserve System*. New York: Ronald Press, 1923.

——. *The Theory and Practice of Central Banking*. New York: Harper, 1936.

Wood, Elmer. *Monetary Control*. Columbia, Missouri: University of Missouri Press, 1963.

Index

Accommodation as a policy guide, 182-184, 201, 227-228
Aldrich, Nelson W., 49-50, 56, 67, 69-72, 74-75, 79
Aldrich Bill of 1908, 49-50
Aldrich Bill of 1911, 67, 69-79, 89, 91, 95-96, 101, 104, 106, 121, 148, 220; relationship to the Federal Reserve Act, 79, 226; uniform rate of discount under, 82, 220
Aldrich-Vreeland Act, 49-51, 62, 115, 177
American Bankers' Association, 43, 53, 87-88, 126
Andrew, A. Piatt, 68, 70, 149-150, 152
Anti-Bullionists, 138-139, 142-143, 147-148
Asset currency, 42, 48, 51, 70, 151; see also Bond-secured currency

Baltimore Plan, 43-46, 143-144; rejection of, 49
Bank of England, 140, 156, 162-170; and the rules of the game, 167-170
Banking School, 142, 147
Bond-secured currency, 42, 68-69; see also Asset currency
Borah, William E., 126-127
Branch banking, 47
Bristow, Joseph L., 128
Bulkley, Robert J., 96, 120
Burke, James F., 122

Call loans, 30, 185

Canadian banking system, 47-49
Captive trust companies, 102
Centralization: debate over, 118-119, 127-131; need for, 206-208
Chase, Salmon P., 20, 38
Clearinghouses, 27-28, 31, 73; loan certificates, 31
Coe, George S., 38
Commercial banking, 18-20, 102
Commercial paper, 52, 59, 66, 154, 187-188; single-name, 20, 158; two-name, 19-20, 55, 155-162; see also Government securities
Committee of Governors on Centralized Execution of Purchases and Sales of Government Securities by Federal Reserve Banks, 224; see also Governors' Committee
Competition for power within the system, 209, 213-219, 222
Conference of Governors, 215-216
Credit Reform School, 148-153
Crises in banking, 27-29
Cunliffe Committee Report of 1918, 164

Davison, Henry P., 70-75, 208
Direct action, 204
Discount rate, 163-164, 190, 193, 219-220; effectiveness of, 166; kept artifically low, 190-191
Divisional reserve banks, 61, 65, 92-93, 95, 103-104, 221-222

Emergency currency, 50-51

Banking Reform and the
Federal Reserve, 1863–1923

Designed by R. E. Rosenbaum.
Composed by York Composition Company, Inc.,
in 11 point Linotype Electra, 3 points leaded,
with display lines in monotype Deepdene.
Printed letterpress from type by York Composition Company
on Warren's Number 66 text, 50 pound basis.
Bound by John H. Dekker & Sons, Inc.
in Columbia book cloth
and stamped in All Purpose foil.

Library of Congress Cataloging in Publication Data
(For library cataloging purposes only)

West, Robert Craig, 1947–
  Banking reform and the Federal Reserve, 1863–1923.

  Bibliography: p.
  Includes index.
    1. Federal reserve banks—History.   2. Banks and banking—United
States—History.   I. Title.
HG2563.W38   1977   332.1'1'0973   76-28028
ISBN 0-8014-1035-5